PN
1978
.C5
S7
1984

Stalberg, Roberta
   Helmer.

China's puppets

$29.95

SEP 3 0 1988	DATE		

© THE BAKER & TAYLOR CO.

CHINA'S PUPPETS

CHINA BOOKS San Francisco

CHINA'S PUPPETS

Roberta Helmer Stalberg

First Edition, 1984

Library of Congress Catalog Card Number: 84-45318
ISBN 0-8351-1372-8
Printed in the United States of America

Book and cover design: Katherine Monahan/Associates

Drawings by: Arlene Lee, Cheryl Nufer and Yu Zheguang.

Photos courtesy of: American Museum of Natural History; Asia Society—Performing Arts Department; Center for Puppetry Arts Atlanta, GA—Mary Carolina Pindar; *China Reconstructs* Magazine; Johan Elbers; Christiane Farcache; Beate Gordon; Longxi Hand Puppet Troupe; Musee Kwok On—A. Fleischer; *National Geographic* Magazine; Pan Yuancheng; Ron Rigo; Christopher Stalberg, M.D.; Roberta Helmer Stalberg; Emma Warfield; Xinhua News Agency—Wang Zijin; and Yang Bizhong.

CONTENTS

Map of China

Turpan

Taklimakan Desert

Zhuozhou
(Zhuo County)

Beijing

Luanzhou
(Luan County)

Tangshan

Laixi County

Yangzhou

Xianyang
Xian

Nanjing

Shanghai

Yilong County

Hangzhou

Chengdu

Longyan Region

Chongqing

Zhangzhou

Yiyang County

Quanzhou

Changsha

Zhangpu County

Shanghang County

Zhaoan County

Meixian Region

Chaozhou

Shantou

Hainan Island

Lufeng County

Longchuan County

Hong Kong

PREFACE

I would like to express my gratitude to the many people in the United States and China who offered helpful suggestions about this book, and especially to: Beate Gordon, Director of the Asia Society's Performing Arts Department, who was instrumental in bringing the subject to my attention through her arrangements with the Chinese People's Association for Friendship with Foreign Countries to bring the Longxi Hand Puppet Troupe for a U.S. performing tour in 1980; to Bettie Erda, who facilitated my access to relevant materials at the American Museum of Natural History; to Nancy Lohman Staub, Vice President, l'Union Internationale de la Marionnette, and Emma Warfield, both dedicated and enthusiastic puppeteers; and to the Center for Puppetry Arts for undertaking the travelling exhibition of Chinese puppets and shadow figures which grew out of the research for this book. I also want to thank Derk and Galia Bodde for their generous permission to study their fine collection of Chinese shadow figures. My thanks go to the staff of China Books & Periodicals for all their help and to Su-hung Chu for the calligraphy which appears in the glossary. Thanks are also due to the kind friends who contributed selected photographs which appear in the book.

I am indebted to the many Chinese puppeteers and researchers who graciously provided me with information and background materials: to Yu Zheguang, President of the Chinese Puppetry and Shadow Theatre Association; to Pan Yuancheng and the China Art Puppet Troupe of Beijing; to the Quanzhou Marionette Troupe; to the Shanghai Puppet Troupe; to Shen Jisheng of the Fujian Drama Research Institute; and to Ada of the Shanghai Animation Film Studio.

This book is dedicated to the Longxi Hand Puppet Troupe, whose exacting performance standards and pursuit of excellence have done much to sustain the art of Chinese puppetry. My special thanks go to those troupe members with whom I travelled in 1980 during their U.S. tour—Jin Nengdiao, Yang Feng, Chen Jintang, Zhuang Huoming, Zhuang Chenhua, Zhu Yalai, and Xu Lina.

I also want to thank my husband, Christopher, who has travelled with me throughout China and took many of the photographs in this book. His constant support, encouragement, and enthusiasm have helped bring this work to completion.

Roberta Helmer Stalberg
New York, New York
July 19, 1984

CHRONOLOGY
OF CHINESE DYNASTIES

Xia (Hsia) Dynasty ca. 21st–16th centuries BC

Shang (Yin) Dynasty ca. 16th century–1066 BC

Zhou (Chou) Dynasty ca. 1066–256 BC
Western Zhou (Chou) / ca. 1066–77 BC
Eastern Zhou (Chou) / 770–256 BC
Spring and Autumn Period / 772–481 BC
Warring States Period / 403–221 BC

Qin (Ch'in) Dynasty 221–206 BC

Han Dynasty 206 BC–AD 220
Western Han / 206 BC–AD 23
Eastern Han / 25–220

Three Kingdoms Period* 220–316
State of Wei / 220–65
State of Shu / 221–63
State of Wu / 222–80

Western Jin (Tsin) Dynasty 265–316

**Eastern Jin (Tsin) Dynasty and
Sixteen States** 317–439
Eastern Jin (Tsin) / 317–420
Sixteen States / 304–439

Southern and Northern Dynasties 386–581
SOUTHERN DYNASTIES
Song (Sung) 420–79
Qi (Ch'i) 429–502
Liang / 502–57
Chen (Ch'en) / 557–89
NORTHERN DYNASTIES
Northern Wei / 386–534
Eastern Wei / 534–50
Northern Qi (Ch'i) / 550–77
Western Wei / 535–57
Northern Zhou (Chou) / 557–81

Sui Dynasty 581–618

Tang (T'ang) Dynasty 618–907

Five Dynasties and Ten Kingdoms Period 907–79
Later Liang / 907–23
Later Tang (T' ang) / 923–36
Later Jin (Tsin) / 936–46
Later Han / 947–50
Later Zhou (Chou) / 951–60
Ten Kingdoms / 902–79

Song (Sung) Dynasty 960–1279
Northern Song (Sung) / 960–1127
Southern Song (Sung) / 1127–1279

Liao (Kitan) Dynasty 907–1125

Western Xia (Hsia) Dynasty 1032–1227

Jin (Nurchen) Dynasty 1115–1234

Yuan (Mongol) Dynasty 1279–1368

Ming Dynasty 1368–1644

Qing (Manchu) Dynasty 1644–1911

Republic of China 1912–1949

People's Republic of China Established 1949

*The Three Kingdoms Period, the Western Jin Dynasty, and the Eastern Jin Dynasty and Sixteen States are also known as the Six Dynasties.

FOREWORD

Puppet theater is surely the quintessence of theatricality. The Chinese have developed it into a high art through many centuries. Played in a curtained structure that hides the manipulators, it draws the audience into a magic circle. No idiosyncrasies of the human actor mar the characterizations and there is nothing to deflect attention from the performance. As the playing space is meager one discards all concern for reality and concentrates on the activity of the figures themselves.

It is the manipulator's dexterity, his vocal powers and his store of dialogue that impress the spectator. Constantly challenged to accept these puppets as sentient human beings (and marvelously non-human beings such as gods and demons) the audience enjoys a sense of participation, of cooperation with the unseen master. Spectator and performer have an alliance in creating the illusion that the dolls are alive.

But the relationship between audience and performer is different in the shadow theater. The light goes on behind the screen and another dimension is added. The manipulator of the figures becomes a remote power, mysterious and absolute. China's shadow master, an amazingly versatile entertainer, has close ties with the performers of Thailand, Malaysia and Indonesia, both in his presentation and in the design of his figures.

Coming on the heels of her handsome book, *China's Crafts*, Roberta Stalberg's publication about puppet theater is a welcome and logical sequel. Puppetry is a highly developed expression of Chinese culture, combining as it does the skills of artisan and performer in a folk art of unusual appeal. I am personally grateful for Dr. Stalberg's careful investigations in China and in the literature from which the dramas are derived.

My introduction to Chinese theater occurred in a museum storeroom. It was a startling encounter that changed my life, for I have been devoted to this somewhat arcane subject ever since. I pulled out a tray of rod puppets and beheld a row of tightly packed little painted faces. One had a frog on its nose, the brow of another was marked with bands of black and gold. These were part of a collection made for the American Museum of Natural History in New York in 1902. Dr. Stalberg has described the experiences of Berthold Laufer, whose mission it was to acquire samples of everything vital to Chinese society at the turn of the century.

The rod puppets were only the beginning, I soon discovered. Laufer's acquisitions included tiny finger puppets, hand puppets, marionettes, two sizes of rod puppets, quantities of Beijing shadow figures, heads, scenery, furniture, vehicles, animals and also the dark, sturdy oxhide Hankow figures and exquisite, tiny sheepskin figures said to be from Hangchou. Roberta Stalberg was unable to find any trace of such figures on her trips to China but we are hoping she will be able to bring us word of their use when she returns.

By Bettie Erda,
Scientific Consultant for the
Anthropology Department
of the American Museum
of Natural History.

中国木偶艺术

Three generations of puppet carvers in the Xu family, with master carver Xu Niansong second from left.

In Yilong County, Sichuan Province, a wiry old master puppeteer hefts a five-foot, fifty-pound wood and cloth figure onto a rod connected to his belt and, defying gravity, moves the massive figure to dance and stride as if weightless. In Zhangzhou city, Fujian Province, an intense young virtuoso conducts a proud pair of twelve-inch hand-puppet warriors through an impossibly complex choreography of flashing swords and parried jabs. In Quanzhou city, Fujian, a keen-eyed master marionettist plucks fifteen strings, while below his hands an imposing general strikes a battle stance and then rushes off into combat.

These are only three of the many faces of a master puppeteer in China. The techniques, the roles, the deft maneuvers that must be mastered—all are part of the legacy of a 2,000-year-old craft.

Early puppetry was the shaman's stock-in-trade, of raising spirits from the dead; later forms incorporated the lively acrobatics of medieval Chinese variety shows. Practitioners have always needed equal skill at gesture, dance, speech, and singing, in order to bring to life the legendary figures of Chinese history and literature, and to do so in a way which suggests their timeless and superhuman essence. In unfolding the themes of loyalty and betrayal, love and hatred, jealousy and compassion, the performer summons up great heroes, beauties, sages, and generals before a rapt audience, traditionally largely adult (only in recent years

THE MASTER PUPPETEER 1

72-year old master string puppeteer Lu Zancheng of the Quanzhou Marionette Troupe.

has the puppeteer added to his repertoire stories for children).

The puppeteer has a special place among Chinese performing artists. While practicing an art form closely associated with human drama and sharing many of the same dramatic conventions, the puppeteer is permitted a greater element of fantasy. He can engender all manner of lively creatures such as tigers, horses, and dragons within the confines of his small stage in a way that is impossible on the stage of the human theatre. He may also endow his characters with all kinds of superhuman abilities such as to fly or change shape at will, or to slay a fierce tiger singlehandedly. In effect, there is no limit to the puppeteer's creativity other than his own artistic ability. The audience knows that the figures they watch are not human, but timeless and representational—liberties granted to the puppet would never be permitted to a human actor.

Perhaps most important of all, it is the legacy of generations of master puppeteers to take what appears to be a liability—namely, the restricted size of stage and figures—and transform it into a unique asset. By honing and refining each motion and gesture to its dramatic essence, the puppeteer captures the heart of a scene and makes less seem more. The puppeteer, the Chinese say, "In one breath tells a thousand ancient tales, and with two hands creates the dance of a million soldiers." The puppets prance and spin, stride or stagger across a stage that seems to expand with their every step. To experience such subtlety and economy of motion is to forget all else and see the world encompassed within the width of a sixty-inch stage.

2

A Closer Look at a Young Master

Perhaps no one represents the consummate artistry and driving spirit of the master puppeteer in China today better than Yang Feng, virtuoso and artistic director of the Longxi Prefectural Hand Puppet Troupe in Fujian Province.

Clever, irrepressible, always ready with a joke, Yang Feng is the fifth generation in the venerable Yang family of hand puppeteers. His great-great-grandfather began the performing legacy two hundred years ago during the Qing dynasty. Over the following generations, the family continued to gain in reknown. Yang's father, Yang Sheng, brought worldwide fame to his family and his troupe after the group won a gold medal in international competition in Bucharest in 1960. At twenty-nine years of age, Yang Feng has already gained fame throughout China, becoming the youngest member of the standing committee of the National Dramatists Association and the first puppeteer to attain such status.

Yang has none of the lofty air of a puppet master, which his background might lead one to expect; rather, he brings to mind a popular Chinese puppet character, the Monkey King: he is mercurial, irreverent and witty. Yet his lightheartedness hides a total dedication to craft and an iron concentration which surface during his virtuoso performances. His hands bring to life a host of characters: a mighty tiger bares its teeth in rage and springs to attack, only to lie down and gnaw distractedly at fleas instead; two warriors armed with lances and shields lunge and parry, leap and spin, in an intricately choreographed display of martial arts. And through it all Yang Feng's feet, though never visible, move in measured pace or poise in the stance of an opera performer, as he dances through a performance.

At the Longxi Hand Puppet School, Yang Feng presides like a benign warlord over an afternoon performance by the students, and reveals his sterner side. With his students he is a difficult taskmaster, expecting from them the same care and concentration he demands of himself. The young performers, mostly in their early teens, clearly respect Yang Feng—are even in awe of him. As they perform, Yang

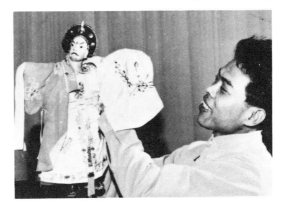

Yang Feng demonstrates his portrayal of the character Luo Dapeng.

watches with intensity, catching every awkward gesture or lapse in rhythm. After the show, he sketches the faults of the whole performance in a few sentences. Despite his youth, he is the artistic heart of the troupe.

Chinese puppeteers, Yang Feng included, are not prima donnas. They follow grueling work schedules and perform under difficult and sometimes crude conditions, especially when they go out into the countryside to perform in farming villages throughout their prov-

A backstage look at the performance of *Furor in the Mandarin's Mansion*.

Yang Feng prepares his tiger for performance.

ince. While dedicated to preserving the traditional spirit of their art, they are at the same time selectively incorporating new techniques and improvements in sound and lighting to heighten the effect of their performances. But let us turn back in time to the puppeteer and the art of earlier ages.

Puppeteers of Traditional China

The earliest form of Chinese puppetry can be traced back over two millennia to the wooden and clay funerary figurines which were placed around the corpse at burial. Such models came into use during the Zhou dynasty (ca. 1066-256 B.C.), replacing the earlier practice of forcing relatives and servants to accompany the deceased in death.

Some of these early wooden mortuary figures were cleverly constructed so that they could move and jump, and seem nearly to come to life. It seems probable that, as part of the funeral rites, a shaman would manipulate the wooden model and make it appear to take on the soul of the deceased. (These practices may have evolved from a funeral ritual in which masked human performers took part, but the available evidence is too scarce to be conclusive.) After calling the soul into the wooden effigy, the shaman would be able to control the soul's wanderings and guide the dead person through the terrors of the underworld safely to heaven. The deceased spirit's travels were no doubt interpreted by appropriate movements and gestures of the wooden figure.

The connection between a moving figure and the animation of the dead is also made in a popular legend transmitted for centuries

4

which purports to record the origin of shadow figures in China. According to legend, in the second century B.C., Emperor Wu of the Han dynasty, heartbroken at the death of his wife, Lady Li, searched for a way to bring her back to him. A resident of the state of Qi, a Taoist magician named Shao-weng, said that he could do this, and one night set up a curtain, candles and a lantern. As the emperor sat in the darkness, his wife's image appeared behind the gauze curtain. The sight of her alleviated his sadness, so that night after night the emperor watched in the darkness as her spirit seemed to appear to him.

Up until the end of the Eastern Han (A.D. 25-220), movable funeral figures were used as part of the death rites, and they were made to sing and dance like real people. Their exact purpose, however, is not clear. It is possible that such jointed and moving figures represented the deceased, and through the skills of a shaman, became animated with the spirit of the dead person, summoned back from death. Early Chinese literature, especially during the Han dynasty, contains numerous examples of such invocations of dead souls. Another theory is that the puppet enabled the shaman to conduct the spirit of the dead person safely through the dangers of the underworld to some sort of paradise afterlife. In either case, the coming to life or movement of the puppet signified the return of the spirit. Such skills figure strongly in the repertoire of shamans throughout Asia, Siberia, and the Arctic.

Some scholars have speculated that Chinese puppets originated from the Great Exorcism ceremonies held before the New Year and during funerals to drive away pestilence and evil influences. The exorcist officiating at such

Yang Feng (left) and Chen Jintang of the Longxi Puppet Troupe rehearse *Furor in the Mandarin's Mansion*.

rituals was the *fang-xiang shi*, who wore a bear skin and "four golden eyes" (probably on a mask) which represented his ability to see in all four directions. At the Great Exorcism held on the eve of the New Year, the *fang-xiang shi* would leap about brandishing a lance and shield, doing battle with the various kinds of demons and evil influences which threatened human life. Following the exorcist in his peregrinations were 120 attendants personifying spirit creatures who devoured the demons of

Lei Wanchun fights with the tiger; both puppets are controlled by Yang Feng.

pestilence. At funerals of important persons, an exorcist also presided, proceeding before the coffin on its way to the tomb and expelling all evil forces lingering there. Some researchers have concluded that the funerary and exorcistic rituals just described gradually developed into rituals using animated figures or puppets in place of masked humans.

At issue here is the exact meaning of the earliest term for puppets, *kui-lei*. Some say the term also refers to the rituals performed by masked humans. Sun Kaidi, in his seminal work on the origins of Chinese puppetry, proposed that *kui-lei* were associated with or identical with the *fang-xiang shi* or exorcists mentioned above. While there are certainly associations between early puppetry and shamanistic performances which used masks, the connection between *kui-lei* and *fang-xiang shi* is not likely to be proved one way or another until further information, probably from archaeological research, comes to light.

Over the centuries, puppeteers expanded their calling to include not only funerals, but also auspicious occasions such as weddings and festivals. What had originally been a religious observance developed into a funeral entertainment accompanied by music. From there it was only a short step to entertainment, pure and simple.

Popular Entertainers of the Song Dynasty

During the Song dynasty a large and thriving middle class patronized all the popular entertainments, including many types of puppetry as well as storytelling and informal dramatic skits. The thirteenth century capital city of Lin-an (present day Hangzhou), had a special designated area for such entertainments, and crowds flocked there daily to thrill to the recreation of famous battles, tales of treachery and defeat, and inspiring heroism. Here, in the great covered bazaars of the pleasure quarters (known as the "tile market") outside the gates of the city wall, scholar and soldier, peasant and merchant could stroll among the myriad popular entertainments of the age. Performers of shadow plays and puppet shows projected high-pitched, nasal voices to accompany their stories of crime and ghosts, Buddhist stories, and romances, all of which had richly comic and satirical elements. Near the bridges to the city, small troupes would set up their portable stages gathering large audiences of passersby. There was incredible diversity of entertainments to be enjoyed: mimics of rural dialects and street vendors' cries; tellers of obscene tales; jugglers of bottles, jugs and plates; experts at asking riddles; and orators who made satirical commentaries proving, for example, that Buddha, Lao-zi and Confucius were really women.

The puppeteers who moved within this bustling milieu practiced a hereditary craft passed down within families for generation after generation. As with storytellers and dramatists, puppeteers wrote down the texts of the plays they specialized in and transmitted these script books from father to son. The family's scripts and performing techniques were carefully guarded from outsiders, because this was the source of the family's livelihood.

A second form of protection came in the form of the professional guilds. These guilds oversaw performance standards of members, regulated disputes, gave economic support to

百
子
圖

were hard, or if a troupe lost regular patronage, they travelled from county to county as itinerants. The drum and the reed *suo-na* would echo to call residents to a performance at the market, square, or street corner; afterwards, the performers were happy to receive any donations. It was not a secure life by any means, but the enthusiasm of their audience served as some recompense to the puppeteers.

As puppet shows grew in popularity, sober Confucian officials grew alarmed that puppeters would encourage the people to immoral or seditious acts. That greatest of Confucian scholar-philosophers, Zhu Xi, who laid the basis for the dominance of Neo-Confucian thought in later ages, is even credited as issuing an edict banning all puppet performances within the area he governed. Quite likely, his official opposition only increased the allure of such performances. Certainly puppetry did not decline, and perhaps it is only poetic justice that Zhu Xi himself became a target of satirical puppeteers who, using carved puppets painted in his likeness and dressed in tall hats and wide, flowing sleeves, portrayed him strutting about the stage lecturing on his main concepts of "principle" and "nature."

Not all officials took the view of Zhu Xi. The ninth century governor of Sichuan Province, Cui Anqian, had puppet shows performed in front of his official residence, allowing commoners and soldiers to watch the puppet theatre acts at will. Cui's motivation was probably more than mere amusement, for popular entertainments had long been considered an excellent source of information about the mood of the people and, more specifically, to find out if they were harboring thoughts of rebellion. Zhou dynasty rulers began collect-

their needy, and mediated in any contact with the government. Popular puppeteers could find additional security if they were retained by wealthy merchants or aristocratic families to give private performances, especially at New Year's or other festival times. During such important seasons, exceptional troupes might also be called to perform at court before the emperor. Between engagements the performers might work in tea houses or singing halls throughout the city. Puppet shows were equally welcome in the countryside, and small villages pooled resources to hire a troupe for days of continuous performing. When times

ing popular poems and songs as a means to see into the life of the people and sent plain-clothed agents or "imperial ears" to mingle at country fairs and urban markets listening for talk of discontent. Puppetry and other folk entertainments no doubt provided considerable information, with their earthy humor and satires of corrupt officials or excessive taxation. In fact, in the ninth century a clever rebel used puppetry as a tool in his plot against the empire. Arranging performances as he traveled from county to county, he was able to determine if there was local unrest which could be turned into support for his rebellion.

The early puppeteers needed to be conversant in not only current events, but classical literature as well. The puppeter's art required skill in the ancient speech used in historical pieces. Although most puppeteers were illiterate and unable to read the original texts, they were still able to bring to life the language of the past in their performances. It is quite likely that there were puppeteers who were scholars who had failed in the difficult series of examinations which led to civil appointment; left without employment but with an excellent literary training, drama and puppetry would have been natural sources of livelihood in spite of the much lower social status. During the Yuan dynasty, the Mongol conquerors of China suspended civil service examinations, with the result that many scholars turned to dramatic and performing arts, either as writers or, if they had the talent, as performers. Under the same dynasty, shadow performers were even dispatched to travel along with the Yuan armies on their campaigns to the west, to provide entertainment for the troops. It shows

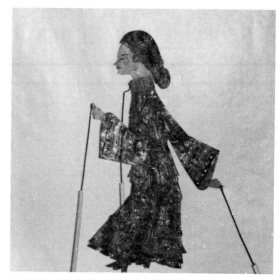

something of the popularity puppet and shadow performances commanded in this age.

Over the centuries puppeteers continued to entertain audiences at rural fairs and town squares, giving special performances to mark festivals, weddings, birthdays, and funerals, or to protect villages in times of famine or epidemic. They passed their performing skills from father to son, preserving their special movements, songs, and scripts and refining them more with each generation. Their performing legacy continues today in China, as young artists give flair to an age-old art form.

Puppetry and Human Drama

Although somewhat outside the scope of this book, we must make some mention of the human drama, of the storyteller, and the connection of these two with the puppet theatre. The stories which unfolded on the puppet stage were, in fact, the same stories which were depicted by human actors or recounted by professional storytellers in marketplace or temple courtyard.

At least as early as the Tang dynasty, professional storytellers had begun to shape the popular oral cycles of myths and historical legends, and by the Song dynasty these tellers of tales competed with shadow and puppet performers for their audiences in the vast amusement parks of the city. They would specialize in only one category of story, the most popular being those drawn from Chinese historical tales, which could be spun on by skillful storytellers for days. The events they recounted were organized into loosely knit episodes which could stand independently or could be grouped into one long, continuous performance, if the audience appeared interested.

By the end of the Song dynasty, storytellers had seen their heyday and were eclipsed by the appearance of fully formed drama. The major subjects of these plays were those of the storyteller—ghosts and the supernatural, history, mystery, and justice; they were of "rouge and powder" (i.e., love stories), knights-errant, and bandit heroes. In addition, such performances not only provided entertainment but passed on essential elements of classical Chinese culture and history in a form understandable by a population which was largely illiterate.

Not only did the puppet and human theatres share a repertoire of plays, but some scholars have suggested that certain dramatic conventions of the human stage can be traced to the puppet theatre. One of these conventions is that actors announce their name and role upon their first appearance on stage. Another is the use of elaborate, mask-like makeup which covers individual features of the human actor and suggests the look of puppets. Third is the stylized and artificial gestures, gait, and postures of human actors that are very reminiscent of shadow and puppet performances. While the exact formative relationship between the shadow and puppet theatres and the human drama is not entirely clear, it is undeniable that these dramatic forms influenced each other, especially in the early years of the development of human drama.

Music, singing and dance or acrobatics were also an important part of both theatres. The use of striking facial designs for certain character types is, as we have seen, another common feature of the human and puppet theatres. Such "painted face" roles reveal their true natures in their faces. *Jing* roles have larger-than-life features and use strong colors symbolic of certain character traits, with red representing courage and honesty, and black indicating unselfishness and justice, for example. *Jing* roles are excessive personality types and their exaggerated facial designs are in keeping with this characteristic. *Chou* roles, on the other hand, are notably deficient in some aspect of their personality. They may lack honesty, self-respect, virtue or courage. White makeup covers their nose, cheeks and sometimes the eyes, drawing attention to the central part of their face and effectively shrinking its size, thus suggesting the *chou*'s deficiency of character.

Current puppet plays fall into several different categories. Traditional stories from mythlogy, history, or literature continue to be very popular, while numerous pieces have been created especially for children. The process of adapting traditional plays or writing new ones is a crucial part of keeping this medium alive, and the puppeteer plays a major role in this work; only he or she knows which events and emotions can be best depicted with puppets. Professional playwrights also take part in this process, and such collaboration can be extremely effective.

One very sucessful adaptation of a traditional play is *Hua Pi* (The Painted Skin), which was originally part of a story in the collection of supernatural tales entitled *A Record of Strange Events Made at Liao Studio*. Written by Pu Songling in the seventeenth century, this collection recounts strange tales of supernatural beings and how they influence and interfere in human affairs. "The Painted Skin" was adapted into a puppet play by Chen Jintang of the Longxi Region Hand Puppet Troupe in 1978, and it has since become one of the troupe's most popular pieces.

The original story was rather complicated, recounting the story of a naive scholar who came under the spell of an evil demon but was finally released from the spell by a Taoist priest. For the puppet stage, the story has been pared to its essence, leaving only three characters. The play conveys the important message that beautiful appearances are not necessarily to be trusted. The piece also shows that the scholar, for all his education, does not have the awareness of good and evil.

Although the human and puppet theatres share certain dramatic conventions and techniques, they have other areas of difference. The puppet and shadow theatres have had more room to develop special effects and miraculous transformations—things which would be impossible in the human drama. Puppet plays pare down the plot to its major theme and limit characters to those who are most important. Because his puppet lacks ability to make complicated facial expressions, the puppeteer uses movement to convey emotion. In the words of master Chinese hand puppeteer Yang Feng, "The art of puppetry is the art of movement."

Puppeteers in China Today

Puppetry has received government support in China since the founding of the People's Republic in 1949. There are today some 90 to 100,000 amateur and professional puppeteers working throughout the country. Like other art

Papercut showing scene from *Monkey Three Times Fights the White Bone Demon*.

forms in modern China, puppetry has been directed to serve the people, meaning, to entertain and raise the cultural level of the large mass of the population rather than to create works appreciated or understood only by a small intellectual elite.

In 1953 a national puppetry art troupe was established in Beijing and some of the country's finest master performers were called to the capital to perform and instruct a younger generation of puppeteers. As further impetus, in 1955 the government directed that a national festival be held for puppeteers from all over the country to encourage improvement of the art. Some 230 puppeteers participated and 53 plays were performed. At that time it was estimated that there were 2,054 puppetry companies and 11,147 pofessional puppeteers in China. By 1966 almost every province and autonomous region had its own professional puppet troupe.

All of these developments ground to a halt in 1966 during the decade known as the Cultural Revolution, when the government launched a vast campaign to eradicate all feudal or counterrevolutionary elements remaining in Chinese art. Because its repertoire was largely made up of traditional stories and legends, the puppet theatre was attacked as being backward and counterrevolutionary. Many provincial companies were dissolved, and some of the great masters underwent bitter persecution during these years. Those troupes which were not dissolved were permitted to perform only the eight model revolutionary operas which Jiang Qing, the wife of Mao Zedong, had promoted. Unfortunately, these were composed of long passages of political discussion, none of which was suitable for performance by puppets—the language of puppetry being its movement, not the spoken word. When puppets were made to mouth long involuted speeches, the performance was lackluster, and even provoked laughter.

By 1976 traditional cultural activities had resumed and the old puppet companies began to be reestablished and perform once again. In 1981 the second national puppetry festival and exchange was held in Beijing and a number of important troupes attended. Such exchanges of information show a marked difference in attitude among performers, who in the past used every means possible to conceal their special techniques from their fellow artists. In 1981 the National Puppetry and Shadow Theatre Association was formed to encourage further development in the art.

Today every province has a professional puppetry company designated as a national or state enterprise; as such they are the most prestigious. These companies are chosen for their high artistic skill and performing standards, and for this honor they have the important responsibility of bringing culture and entertainment to the populace. They also develop educational plays on political or moral themes for children.

There is another important type of professional troupe under collective ownership. These companies are generally smaller than state-level companies and are not accorded the same status; moreover, their performers generally receive lower wages and fewer fringe benefits. They are jointly owned and run by a group, such as a city district, a commune or a production brigade. Of the thirty troupes ac-

The author with members of the Longxi Puppet Troupe and their families.

tive today, most are in cities or regions where puppetry has always been very strong, as in the provinces of Guangdong and Fujian.

In addition to the professional troupes who receive a salary and benefits for year-round performing, there are any number of amateur troupes scattered throughout China, particularly in the countryside, where they divide their work time between farming and puppetry. In this respect their schedule is reminiscent of puppeteers in old China who performed largely during slack agricultural seasons in winter and early spring when peasants had the spare time to attend such entertainments but then disbanded for the rest of the year when there was other employment. To-day's farmer/puppeteers have a stable liveli-hood from their agricultural efforts and perform during leisure winter hours for the entertainment of their family or village. They may receive some money for their show, but the stimulus is personal enjoyment, not profit. It is estimated that there are over one thousand such part-time puppeteers in the mountains of Zhejiang Province alone. Although they may lack the complicated staging and polished technique of the professionals, such rural ama-teurs are usually extremely conservative about

local traditions, and their conservatism has helped to ensure the old arts are not lost.

Cities also do what they can to encourage amateur puppeteers. Shanghai, for example, has three amateur adult troupes as well as training programs for young amateurs. All of these activities are carried out by the Shanghai Puppet Troupe, an important state-level rod puppet company. These programs are a good example of the way modern puppeteers use their art to "serve the people."

What the Future Holds

In the years to come, puppeteers will work to solidify the performing skills of earlier generations while developing new skills. Part of the work of teachers in puppetry schools is to collect and organize traditional oral lore about the art form and about special performing techniques.

Most puppeteers were illiterate before 1949, and without written records, their knowledge was precarious. The irrevocable loss of such information is a tragedy all the more bitter because it was unnecessary. During the Cultural Revolution when classical puppetry virtually disappeared in China, troupes scattered and some of the old master performers died, and as a result, some techniques were lost. Today puppeteers are working to restore these skills and record them so that they will become a secure part of the performing heritage of future generations.

Director and players of the Shanghai Puppet Troupe rehearse a scene from *Monkey Three Times Fights the White Bone Demon.*

In one movement are created the ancient stories
   of a thousand autumns,
Within three feet are engendered ten thousand miles
   of mountains and streams...

     —*Traditional inscription on the
     puppet theatre of Fujian Province*

15

中国木偶艺术

The beginnings of Chinese puppetry lie cloaked in the dust of time. Written records about the art are extremely rare before the twelfth century, and even then the descriptions are so terse as to be tantalizingly vague. The best evidence to emerge about early puppet forms has come from burial figures, placed in tombs as part of the funeral ritual. In recent years, great numbers of funerary figures have been discovered in China, the most extraordinary find of all being the army of life-size terra-cotta soldiers, cavalry, horses, and generals which guarded the flank of the tomb of the First Emperor of the Qin Dynasty (third century B.C.).

Like many other peoples, the early Chinese believed in a very material, concrete afterlife. They buried their dead with all the furnishings, utensils and comforts to which they were accustomed while living. This included, during the Shang dynasty (ca. 16th century-1066 B.C.), slaves or captives of war who were enterred in the tombs of nobles or royalty so that their souls might watch over the grave and serve their masters in death as they had in life. As this custom began to fall into disuse, human sacrifices were replaced by effigies of the servants and attendants. Such figures, called *yong*, were first made of straw and later of clay and wood. Some *yong* came to have moving parts; in condemning these moving funeral figures, Confucius said they were too much like humans and would cause people to treat human sacrifice lightly.

Puppet theatre used for imperial family, late 19th and early 20th century. *(Courtesy of The American Museum of Natural History)*

ORIGINS AND DEVELOPMENT OF CHINA'S PUPPETS 2

Earliest extant Chinese puppet, over 2,000 years old.

Recently an example of such movable figures came to light. In the spring of 1979 a six-foot, two-inch wooden figure was unearthed in Laixi County, Shandong Province. It was found in a tomb dating to the Western Han dynasty, about 107 B.C. Constructed of thirteen main strips of wood, jointed to permit movement of knees, shoulders, and waist, the figure could be made to sit, kneel or stand. The abdomen and legs had been drilled with many holes, which were either of use in attaching strings to control movement or in tying on a costume. A very impressive figure, with long limbs and a solemn expression—with the addition of costume, it must have looked remarkably realistic, even majestic. It is impossible to say exactly how this early puppet was operated—whether by strings or by some more elaborate mechanical device. However, a forty-five-inch long silver rod was also discovered near the figure, and Chinese experts speculate that this may have been used to control the figure's hands and feet. It is notable that the figure comes from Shandong, the ancient state of Qi, a region famous for its magicians, alchemists, and woodworkers or carpenter-engineers. Possibly a little of each of these specialties went into the creation of this figure. Qi was also the home of Shao-weng, the man who, according to legend, brought the Lady Li back to Emperor Wu by constructing one of the earliest shadow figures in China.

Early Written Sources About Puppetry

There are several written sources which claim to record the origins of different forms of Chinese puppetry. The account purporting to be the earliest is the popular legend of the famous craftsman named Master Yan who was said to have lived about 1000 B.C. The story tells us that the craftsman by the name of Yan who was able to construct puppets so perfect in movement that they appeared to be human dancers. The fame of the figures grew and eventually Master Yan was called to perform before the king. When the ruler saw one of the figures wink provocatively at his concubines, however, he grew enraged and ordered that the offending performer be put to death. "Because the dancer is my own son," Master Yan replied, "I would prefer to carry out the execution myself." And so saying, he brought out his puppet and disassembled it before the astonished king, revealing its ingenious inner workings. Needless to say, the king was so impressed that he awarded Master Yan a large sum of gold in appreciation of his creating a new form of entertainment.

An interesting legend, but the 1000 B.C. dating is totally unreliable, as parts of the text in which it occurs were written as late as the third century B.C. Also, the exact kind of figure is unknown; it is possible that it was a kind of automaton or mechanical figure that moved by internal devices rather than direct manual control. Such automatic figures were very popular in China and were capable of an impressive repertoire of movements.

Another account, written in the ninth century A.D., cites movable figures that existed about 200 B.C. According to this story, General Liu Bang (who later was to found the Han dynasty) came under seige by nomadic invaders, the Xiong-nu, from beyond China's western frontiers. One of Liu Bang's ministers, named Chen Ping, had heard that the wife of the nomadic tribe's leader, herself a warrior commanding her own army, had a jealous nature.

戲呱題

A marionette performance, with additional marionettes hanging in the wings. *(Courtesy of The American Museum of Natural History)*

Chen Ping constructed a large wooden figure of a beautiful woman with an internal mechanism which allowed it to dance just like a real person. He displayed it on the city walls, and made it dance within view of the besieging armies. The Xiong-nu leader's wife, seeing the great beauty of this Chinese woman, became afraid of victory, for if the city fell, the beautiful woman would be offered to her husband as a captive. So she retired with the army which she commanded, thus breaking the siege. Although it is an interesting tale, this account, too, is somewhat questionable in the way it is recorded. Earlier sources either mention no figure at all or mention the use of a painted picture rather than a puppet.

For actual documentation of puppet performances, we must wait until the sixth century A.D., even though such performances probably existed earlier. Tang dynasty (A.D. 618-907) literature contains evidence of many types of popular puppet performance, and by the Song dynasty (A.D. 960-1279) long lists existed of the most famous master performers of the era, with stage names such as Lu of the Golden Strings which hinted at their special talents. It is interesting that several of the puppeteers are mentioned as working also as actors in the variety plays of the time, which suggests how close the entertainments were in this age. Of further interest is the fact that of the performers whose names have come down to us, a few were women, such as Sixth Sister Zu, Second Sister Li, and Mother Hei. All of them are listed as performers of shadow plays. This raises tantalizing questions about the participation of women in medieval Chinese puppetry, but unfortunately, any answers to those questions must await the discovery of new sources. At any rate, it is certain that the society of Tang and Song China was far more open for women than it was in later centuries; women were eventually barred from performing in drama or puppet performances. It was not until 1949 that they began to re-emerge as puppeteers.

By the eleventh century, documents confirm that the popularity of puppeteers was widespread and their performances enjoyed by emperor and peasant alike. One anecdote from the eleventh century writer Zhang Le relates an extreme case. A wealthy but apparently very naive young orphan living in the capital loved shadow plays above all else. As he watched a performance of *The Romance of the Three Kingdoms* in which a heroic general named Guan Yu is slain, he cried out for the puppeteer to delay the death. Unfortunately for the young man, the crew was an unscrupulous group of ne'er-do-wells, who saw a chance to squeeze out a tidy payment. The shadow performer told the young man that he was afraid to bring Guan Yu to his end because his ghost would be fierce and might do harm to those involved in the death. In order to avoid endangering their lives, the puppeteer suggested that the orphan hold a sacrificial banquet after the performance in which Guan Yu was slain and thereby appease the spirit. This idea appealed to the young innocent, who gave money to the puppeteer to purchase the finest wine and meat for the sacrifice which was, of course, attended by the whole lot of hangers-on. Nor did their imposition end here, as they prevailed upon the young man to divide up the silver sacrificial vessels among

them. The moral of the story is clear and reinforces the lingering stigma attached to performers in general throughout Chinese history.

Puppetry becoming an Art Form

The connection between puppetry and funeral celebrations in China continued up to the twentieth century. But it was only a matter of time before the entertainment spread to other settings; as early as the second century, puppets were a part of parties, weddings, and happy occasions of all sorts. The exact substance of such entertainments is not known, but one may guess that they were informal skits including dance and movement as basic features, performed with singing and musical accompaniment and liberal doses of comedy and satire. By the sixth century these humorous puppetry performances using characters made of wood were popular with the Emperor Gao Wei, the last ruler of the northern state of Qi. This emperor was an extravagant ruler whose excesses went far towards bringing the final downfall of his dynasty. The puppetry show popular at this time centered around a jesting acrobatic slapstick character who was fat and bald, named Guo Gong or Lord Guo; he was also called Bald Guo. Guo Gong can also be translated as "the Duke of Guo," and because Guo denotes a feudal domain in the ancient northeastern state of Qi, the name connects the art to this region. The contents of this puppetry entertainment preserved the elements of song and dance used earlier, and revolved around the antics of Bald Guo. He was the leading player and introduced the show with witty comic remarks. So important was the character of Guo Gong that his name became synonymous with the show in which he starred and even to puppetry in general.

During the eighth century, puppetry once again found a place at court, this time under the patronage of the Emperor Xuan-zong, who is revered as the patron deity of all Chinese drama. At his palace in Changan (present day Xian), he established a school for training young boys and girls in music, dance, and dramatic entertainments. Because the school was located in a pear garden, in later years actors referred to themselves as "children of the Pear Garden." We know the emperor held the puppet theatre in high regard because he had teaching quarters for puppetry and other folk entertainments installed within the palace.

Despite his brilliance as a patron of the arts, Xuan-zong was less lucky in matters of government, and his fascination for the extravagant consort Yang Guifei and inattention to the practical concerns of ruling led to the disastrous An Lushan rebellion, his flight from the capital, and his tacit consent to the execution of his consort before his eyes. In his later years he was a saddened man and he used the poignant metaphor of a string puppet to express his powerlessness:

With carved wood and stretched silk
threads, this old man is made,
with aged skin chicken-like and hair like a
crane's, he is just like a real man;
In a moment, the manipulation finished,
he lies still and at rest—
Just like man's life within this world of dreams.

This poem tells us more. From it we know that string puppets were used at least by the eighth century, and probably were not a form used in the rolicking Guo Gong farces. String puppetry is not well suited to fast acrobatics, and it is more likely that some kind of rod puppetry was used to animate Guo Gong.

In the following Song dynasty, dramatic performances and puppetry attained an unprecedented variety and popularity. This development owes much to the emergence at this time of thriving urban centers with a large middle class which could afford to patronize such entertainments year-round, giving performers a reasonably reliable living. Comic variety shows employing political satire and bawdy humor emerged as an important form in this period, as did the storyteller's art of spinning out episodic recitals day after day in front of temple or marketplace. The puppet theatre shared elements with these other folk forms in the eleventh and twelfth centuries, when competition kept performers alert to the many dramatic techniques used by their competitors which could be put to advantage in their own puppet medium.

Early Types of Puppets

But what types of puppets entertained the people of old China? There were five forms of the art in practice by the tenth century, and these have formed the basis of all styles seen today, although some are no longer in use. One other type, hand puppets, appeared in China in the sixteenth century.

String puppets are worked from above by means of strings attached to the body, arms, legs, feet, and hands. One of the earliest forms of puppetry, it still flourishes today.

Head of a young man, southern Chinese rod puppet theatre 19th century. *(Photo: A Fleischer, courtesy Musee Kwok On)*

Rod puppets are manipulated by a central wood or bamboo stick which controls the body of the puppet, with secondary rods controlling arm movements. Oral tradition dates its origin to the Tang dynasty.

Water puppets seemed to be of some importance in Song times and were frequently used in imperial entertainment. We know that they were performed from a floating stage in a pond or lake, while the audience watched from nearby boats or from the shore. Their appearance and movement are not exactly known; they may have been elaborate mechanical figures powered by the water current. Or, they may have been manipulated puppets, controlled from beneath the water. The form has disappeared in China but one type has remained popular in Vietnam, presumably introduced there during the centuries of Chinese influence.

Flesh puppets (or "puppets in the flesh") appear to have been a reversal of art imitating life: small children would stand on an adult's shoulders and act roles as well as sing and dance. The form lost popularity over the centuries, probably because such performances were limited in length and complexity. For the past one hundred years a similar form of short folk drama called "shoulder theatre" has been performed in Fujian Province. It is assumed this practice migrated from central China where it was once popular. Some scholars speculate that one form of flesh puppet *(rou kuei-lei)* of the Song dynasty was a forerunner of the hand puppet. More of a children's game, where the fingers were painted and clothed to resemble characters, it was a far cry from the true hand puppetry that existed in the Ming and Qing dynasties.

Shadow figures are two-dimensional figures that move behind a silk or nylon screen illuminated from the rear. At first such figures were cut from plain paper; later, they were made from leather and then colored to give them greater beauty and durability. During the Song dynasty there were also performances of "large shadow shows" (*da-ying xi*) in which human actors moved like shadow figures. Such shows may have been exclusively connected with the lantern festival which falls on the fifteenth of the first month, according to the lunar calendar, and marks the culmination of two weeks of celebration of the new year.

While out of the direct scope of this book, *automatic or mechanical figures* deserve mention. Such figures have been extremely popular in China for centuries, with emperors and peasants alike. Some accounts of movable figures could actually be of automatic rather than hand-manipulated figures. One description from the third century A.D. tells of a complete mountain constructed of wood and covered with a myriad of figures powered by water and performing the "hundred entertainments," such as singing, dancing, acrobatics, juggling, wrestling, magic, and masquerades. Some of these automated pageants were very elaborate, especially those for the emperor. In the seventh century, for example, Emperor Yang of the Sui dynasty, witnessed a procession of seventy-two pageants recreating the important events in Chinese history and mythology, all performed by wooden automatic figures about two-feet high and operated by water flow.

The development of such intricate and elaborate figures was, of course, beneficial to the puppeteer and his art. He was able to ex-

Carved heads for rod puppets at the Hunan Rod Puppet Troupe workshop in Changsha.

tract certain techniques and construction experience which no doubt helped to improve puppet forms and add to his skills. Both automated figures and hand-manipulated puppets were to provide cross currents of influence and competition for centuries.

Current Types of Puppets

Most performers in China today are active in rod puppetry. The China Art Puppet Troupe in Beijing and the Shanghai Puppet Troupe are both large, state-level companies with rod puppet specialists numbering in the hundreds. They are among the most prestigious rod troupes in China, along with the provincial puppet troupes of Hunan and Guangdong. In addition there are a number of younger rod puppet troupes throughout the country, even in areas where puppetry has not been a traditional form of entertainment, such as in the

23

Hand puppeteer holds figure of a scholar.

Guizhou Autonomous Region, Heilongjiang Province and Inner Mongolia.

String puppetry today is found mainly along the Chinese coast in the provinces of Jiangsu, Zhejiang, Fujian, and Guangdong, as well as in the Western province of Sichuan. In these areas, marionette performances are a part of popular tradition that has been kept alive. Quanzhou, Fujian Province, is the famous old port city from which Marco Polo left

China on his return voyage to Venice. The Quanzhou troupe is probably the most famous marionette troupe in China, renowned for executing difficult movements in a fluid and elegant style. Their special techniques will be discussed further in Chapter Four.

Hand puppetry continues to be very popular in the southeastern province of Fujian, where it has flourished for at least 500 years. The province today has two large and prestigious hand puppet companies in the cities of Zhangzhou and Quanzhou. A number of amateur troupes also perform throughout the province. Chinese hand puppetry is also performed in Hong Kong and Taiwan.

The art of shadow theatre continues to be popular in the northern Chinese areas of Hebei, Shaanxi, and Shanxi provinces, in Harbin and Tangshan, as well as in Sichuan, Hunan, and Guangdong provinces. The Hunan Provincial Shadow Troupe is considered one of the best modern shadow companies. Tangshan in Hebei Province, also long renowned for its shadow theatre, has evolved a special kind of music that is used only in the shadow performances.

Puppetry in modern China is a living tradition, and formalized training has ensured that the new generation of puppeteers will produce its share of master performers.

中国木偶艺术

Young puppet carver creating heads for a variety of hand puppet characters.

In southern China, the dramatic art of "the cloth bag theatre"—hand puppetry—has been passed from father to son for generations with a conservatism and respect for traditional detail that is unequalled in the country.

The people of Fujian are fiercely proud of their cultural heritage, rightfully boasting that much of their art and theatre predates any in the north, where early traditions were supplanted by foreign invasions of the Mongols, and later the Manchus. As an example, the local dialect of southern Fujian, called *min-nan hua*, is one of the most archaic of Chinese dialects, traceable to a form of early Chinese carried south over seventeen centuries ago. Popular culture is also remarkably enduring here, where texts of ancient novels written over a thousand years ago are still common knowledge.

Fujian has long been an important center for Chinese puppetry, and particularly hand puppet theatre; one might even call it the heart of classical Chinese puppetry. And for this reason, although hand puppetry of other regions must be mentioned, our focus will be on the cloth bag theatre of Fujian.

The Cloth Bag Theatre of Fujian

Hand puppetry in Fujian goes by several names: "cloth bag theatre;" "theatre within the palm," and "art on the palm." The beautiful, little puppets used in Fujian are constructed around a cotton glove shell forming

HAND PUPPETS 3

the upper body, into which the puppeteer's hand is inserted to control the figure. The lower body consists of cotton-stuffed legs with carved wooden feet which are stitched on to the upper body shell. To the ends of the empty sleeves are attached carved hands which may be adjusted to hold props. The carefully carved and painted head is hollow to permit control by the puppeteer's forefinger. The head is removeable and may be interchanged with different puppet bodies.

Hand puppets are believed to have appeared in the sixteenth century, creations of a Fujian scholar who wanted to publicly protest against the treachery of the eunuch Wei Zhongxian. The first figures measured about eight inches, with heads an average of one and one-half inches. In the last fifty years, however, master puppeteers have enlarged the size of the bodies to fourteen inches and heads to two and one-half inches to increase the dramatic effect and visibility so that performances could be given to larger audiences. This change has affected the puppet stage as well. Puppeteers at one time used an elaborately carved wooden puppet stage that had two levels. On the lower level were three doors hung with silk curtains, and on the upper level were three large windows covered with movable wooden panels. The stage was about six feet wide, seven feet high, and four feet deep.

This early puppet stage could accommodate two seated puppeteers at any one time, with each artist frequently manipulating two puppets simultaneously. The master performer was called the *tou-shou* (leading hand) or *ding-shou* (upper hand), while his assistant was called the *er-shou* (second hand), *zhu-shou* (helping hand), or *xia-shou* (lower hand). Dur-

ing the course of a play, a puppeteer might enact five or six characters, including movement and all voice parts. The "first hand," or master puppeteer performed the major roles, while the "second hand," who was still an assistant performer and usually an apprentice, only performed minor roles and did not have speaking or singing parts.

In 1952 the old-style theatre of seated performers was replaced; a larger, more open stage now permits ten or more artists to perform at the same time. Modern features such as taped music and special lighting have also been selectively adopted to enhance the dramatic effect of the performance.

Special Features of Classical Fujian Theatre

The hand puppet theatre is famous for its fast pace and realistic action. Its puppet characters are clothed in the same costumes and sport the same mask-like features as the human opera. Dance, song, and musical accompaniment are also much the same. A puppet warrior, for example, can be recognized by its bright silk gown worked front and back with elaborate embroidery depicting a ferocious tiger, to symbolize the strength and valor of a general. On its head is a high, rounded hat denoting rank. The character's personality is clearly revealed (to an informed audience) by the face makeup: red denoting bravery, black for loyalty, and white showing cunning or treachery.

This form of puppetry lends itself to the swift and abrupt movements required in acrobatics and martial arts, and it is not surprising that these should be among the theatre's specialties. In such scenes, a puppeteer controls one puppet with each hand, perfectly coordinating jabs and parries, spins and jumps. The hand puppet form is also excellent for portraying animals, and the Fujian puppeteers are famed for their lifelike characterization of tigers and horses.

The play, *Lei Wanchun Fights the Tiger*, popular in southern China, demonstrates the unique capabilities of the hand puppet theatre. In this traditional piece, a scholar on his way to take the civil service examinations stops overnight at an inn. The scholar's page, overhearing that the innkeeper plans to rob and murder his master, warns him and they flee in terror.

The hero, Lei Wanchun, is now introduced as he lurches on stage in an advanced stage of intoxication. He begins to sink down and then slowly pulls himself up by his long spear anchored in the ground before him. In this state, he decides to go up on the mountain and look for a tiger said to be terrorizing the region. He leaves brandishing his spear. Offstage, the roar of a tiger is heard. In one giant leap, a tiger throws himself onstage where he grimaces and

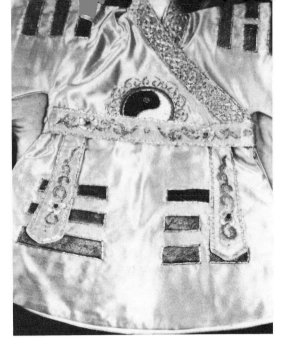

The resplendent costume of a Daoist priest, with cosmic diagram of the eight trigrams and the yin-yang symbol.

Close-up look at the padded, thickly embroidered costume of a warrior, with couching in gold thread.

The scholar and his assistant come on stage. Note the silk sleeves which blend with the puppets' costume. Performers are Zhu Yalai (left) and Xu Lina (right).

tosses his head in a display of untamed power. In a moment his mood shifts, and he forgets his majesty to gnaw distractedly at a flea on his side. Finally having overcome the flea, the tiger lolls his head and flicks his tail up to bounce against his ear in lazy contentment, like the most docile of cats. This is a strikingly effective scene, revealing two very different personalities of the tiger in a transition which is also extremely humorous. The mood changes once again as the scholar is surprised by the tiger's challenging roar. Caught between the tiger and the pursuing innkeeper, the scholar cries that all hope is lost. At this crucial moment, Lei Wanchun emerges to confront the tiger. The two figures (performed by one puppeteer) surge and pivot with primitive strength, as well-matched adversaries. In the heat of combat, Lei Wanchun throws off his outer coat to free himself for better movement—an impressive maneuver impossible to perform with any other type of puppet. After another sequence of wild combat, the tiger is overcome and impaled on Lei Wanchun's spear.

Another adversary still remains, however. The innkeeper and his henchmen stride onstage. In a second fierce struggle, the hero matches the blows of the three villains until first the innkeeper deserts, and then his henchmen. Lei Wanchun, joined by his niece and assistant, overcomes the three villains to the great gratitude of the scholar and his page.

This play employs all of the special skills of the Fujian hand puppeteer—martial arts and acrobatics, difficult maneuvers, and vivid animal portrayals. Another highlight of the play is its sophisticated dramatic pace, ranging from the sluggish motion of the drunken hero and the indolent scratching of the tiger to the swift

fighting scenes, all punctuated by stationary tableaux at key moments.

The role of the tiger is very popular, and a strong Chinese folk image. The tiger in its natural state is beautiful, standing with tail erect, then twisting his body to right and left while quivering with power. This characterization was especially developed by the Longxi Regional Hand Puppet Troupe under the tutelage of the master puppeteer Yang Sheng, and further adapted by his son Yang Feng.

Another striking aspect of this episode is the relationship between Lei Wanchun and the tiger. Both are powerful, commanding figures and each in his way stands outside the social order—the tiger because he is a wild creature and Lei Wanchun because, despite his assistance to his fellows, he is too independent to be subject to society's strictures. His primitive exuberance is further pointed up by his improper fondness for drink. Folk culture often idolizes such rebel heroes who are honest,

Lei Wanchun slays the tiger; both puppets are controlled by Yang Feng.

brave, and strong, but too independent to reach high rank or acceptance within society.

Control and Basic Movements

The hand puppet is controlled by the forefinger supporting the head, with the thumb forming one arm and the middle, ring, and little fingers forming the other arm. It is essential to maintain a ninety-degree angle between forefinger and middle finger so that the shoulders of the puppet appear realistically level. This position is difficult, and puppeteers must begin training while still young, before the tendons of the hand have become inflexible. To train the hand into this unnatural position the puppeteer stretches his forefinger and middle finger into a right angle against a table edge or some other rigid surface. He will repeat this exercise, depending on his level of training, at least once a day with both hands.

A second basic type of control calls for the ring and little fingers to be flexed in toward the palm. This permits movement of the waist and chest of the puppet from within the costume sheath.

At most times the fingers are kept spread so that the hands of the puppet appear to hang in a natural way; if the fingers are allowed to close, the puppet will appear awkward, with its arms raised overhead.

To achieve total naturalism, the puppeteer must have perfect control of all finger movements and be able to move each finger independently of the others. The forefinger must be perfectly steady, or the puppet's head will appear to wobble right and left most unnaturally. It is an art that demands equal agility and control in both hands for directing martial arts sequences and other action scenes.

In another basic movement, the thumb moves out of the sleeve into the body of the costume and grips the lower rim of the puppet head against the forefinger in order to move the head up and down or turn it in any direction. Motions of the head, although uncomplicated, require great subtlety and a lightness of movement appropriate for the puppets' size. The smallest movement is enough to convey deep emotions, such as a head sunk down lost in thought, or a shy glance from a modest young girl.

The legs and feet are moved by the puppeteer's free hand or, if he is already manipulating a second puppet, the manipulation is done by another puppeteer.

Special Techniques

The master hand puppeteers of Fujian have developed a number of impressive performance techniques. The special demands and capabilities of their puppets have dictated the development of the performing art, evolving dramatic features that no other puppet form has. The essential distinction is always that in hand puppetry, the joints and bones of the puppeteer's hand directly produce form and movement in the figure. Other puppet forms create motion and substance via outside or indirect control sources, such as strings or rods. Only hand puppetry requires a direct relationship between the figure and the hand.

Hand puppet ready for action, forefinger supporting the head and thumb and fingers, the two arms.

Controlling the head movement with thumb and fingers.

Hand puppet theatre is also special in the sense of strength which is conveyed through the control of legs and feet. During martial confrontations, the feet are spread in a challenging and aggressive stance, and figures stride and stagger across the stage. This motion is not possible for string puppets, whose feet are controlled by strings from above and cannot be anchored on stage; when they walk they move slowly or float lightly across the stage. Rod puppets in most cases do not even have feet, and so their stance can only be suggested by the fall of a garment.

Probably the most famous element of the Fujian hand puppet theatre is its performance of martial arts. The small figures brandish spears, shields, and swords, flashing them faster than the eye can see, each blow registered by the staccato ring of wooden prop against wooden prop. Weapons and other objects are held in two ways, depending on the character; warrior puppets have carved fists

The acrobats who juggle plates in the play *Da-Ming Prefecture*.

Two different types of carved hands: right is used for martial plays and left for civil plays without strenuous fighting scenes.

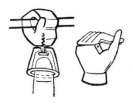

with a central opening through which a spear or sword can be securely inserted. A more flexible method is used for other characters, such as women or officials, whose articulated hands are jointed. When their role calls for them to carry a parasol or hold a pipe, a rubber band is used to secure the object within the palm.

A combat scene may have as many as ten figures crowding the stage, and their precisely choreographed confrontation will be under the control of five puppeteers.

Special techniques add to the drama of martial arts scenes. Sometimes a hand puppet will spin around in a swift circle by pivoting on the performer's forefinger. Sometimes a puppet will fly up into the air and disappear offstage after having been cast off the performer's hand; this action is seen frequently in today's *kung-fu* movies as warriors appear to fly from spot to spot. Far more difficult is the action in which a puppet flies up and then lands on the stage to perform again with no break in dramatic rhythm. This sequence requires sure control and long hours of practice, as one puppeteer casts the puppet upward off his hand and another performer catches it with forefinger extended. Not only must the receiving puppeteer catch the puppet, but he or she must also be conscious of the height of the stage and not extend his hand where it can be seen by the audience. Conversely, he must not hold his hand too low, or the puppet will disappear from view; the catch must be made precisely at stage level.

Audiences are also amazed to see hand puppets performing tricks a human juggler might do. They will balance spinning plates, with the help of an L-shaped metal rod with

two vertical extensions, inserted into the puppet's mouth. The puppet throws a plate into the air and catches it on the shorter rod, spinning the plate faster and faster until it becomes completely horizontal. There are no hidden wires or strings to balance or control the plate, which the puppeteer then casts up in the air and catches on the longer rod. Then a second plate is tossed from offstage and this is caught on the other rod so that both plates are now spinning together. Now for the one secret in this trick: a slight indentation in the base of the plates helps the puppeteer control their spin and keeps them from slipping.

It is a particular feature of Chinese opera—both human and puppet—to balance motion and stillness by including abrupt tableaux in which the figures poise with arms extended and one leg raised with knee bent. These dramatic postures serve to focus and intensify the audience's emotion at key moments in a play. The same effect is employed in human drama and many drama experts, in fact, theorize that such opera postures derived from early puppet performances.

Perhaps the most distinctive feature of a Fujian hand puppet performance is the striking vitality which the figures exude. During international performances in Paris, Bucharest, and Australia, the Longxi Hand Puppet Troupe was besieged by members of the audience who were unable to believe that the puppets were not powered by hidden electronic or mechanical devices. Over the centuries southern Chinese puppeteers have evolved a number of special methods to create this extraordinary realism. One of the simplest techniques is the puppeteer's ability to keep a puppet (or puppets) in constant motion on stage. Warriors stride back and forth, shy beauties look down and sway gently, fawning sycophants bow and hover obsequiously around a high official. A puppet never stands motionless on stage unless it is done deliberately during a dramatic tableau. Human actors can afford to remain still because the audience never doubts they are alive; with puppets, the illusion of life must always be maintained.

This brings us to another important principle of the hand puppeteer's art. The classical hand puppet theatre of South China is not an art which bases itself upon realism. Rather, the hand puppets must be *more real* than living people; only by exaggeration can the puppeteer convey a feeling of realism. This holds true for all forms of Chinese puppets, but especially so for the hand puppet theatre of Fujian. Because the hand puppets are six to eighteen inches smaller than other types of Chinese puppets, every gesture, every motion must be imparted with maximum effect. All nonessentials are excised so as not to distract from the essential motif or story line, which is, as a result, amplified larger than life.

Fifth-generation puppeteer Yang Feng has likened this art to the poet's struggle to strip complex ideas and feelings down to their most basic and compelling images. He terms this process *mu-ouhua* or "puppetization." It requires that the master performer study people, animals, motions, or even events and perceive their artistic heart or dramatic essence; this can then be realized in physical terms in whatever way best suits the unique capabilities of a puppet performance. The artistic vision of Yang Sheng and his son, Yang Feng, in creating the unforgettable persona of a tiger in *Lei Wanchun Fights the Tiger* exemplifies this process of *mu-ouhua*. Through the artist's efforts, subtle feelings or characteristics are conveyed in visible, physical form.

How does a puppet communicate strength or courage, for example? While using concrete details of the puppet such as large, glaring eyes and a painted face, the puppeteer has reduced the quality of "strength" to one simple physical gesture: when faced with a challenge, the warrior's whole body vibrates convulsively, establishing his barely restrained power. In another dramatic moment, to communicate the stress of fierce combat, two adversaries will move apart momentarily to thrust chests forward and backward as if panting for breath. This movement is also used at the end of an energetic lion dance when the lion costume is cast aside and the two puppet "lion dancers" emerge from the belly of the costume, swaying rhythmically to portray the

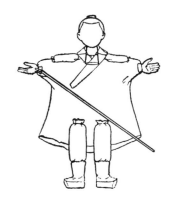

Small interior rod inserted into the puppet's hand in order to control movements of a prop such as a fan.

Poem and calligraphy by the well-known scholar, Guo Moruo, in praise of brilliant performing.

lions' forced breathing after the dance.

The dramatic scene of combat in the story of Lei Wanchun and the tiger also features this movement, and the reason for its use in this particular play is interesting. In 1956, during a performance in Paris, Yang Sheng was controlling the two puppets of Lei Wanchun and the tiger. Just before the tiger was to make a terrific leap to attack the hero, the puppeteer discovered that the tiger's foot had become caught in a narrow crack in the floor of the puppet stage. As both his hands were already in use, he could not disentangle the foot, nor could he get the attention of the other performers to help

him. In order to stall for time, he held the two puppets on stage in place and caused them to pant for breath. The audience was delighted, and gave forth a burst of applause which finally caught the attention of the other performers since there was not supposed to be anything special occurring at that moment. The foot was freed and the play concluded, but Yang Sheng was so pleased with the effect of his impromptu change that he incorporated it permanently into the play.

All of these details add up to evoke an extraordinary illusion of blood and bone, of life force. With an unerring sense of drama, the master hand puppeteer creates scenes of such disturbing realism that it is easy to understand why local lore recounted stirring tales of puppets come to life.

Backstage Preparations

In order to complete their difficult maneuvers smoothly and successfully, Chinese puppeteers carefully arrange the backstage area with all puppets and props to be used in a play. Although this part of a performance is never seen by the audience, it is as crucial to the finished dramatic effect of a play as are the long hours of practice. All puppets are laid out according to when and where they appear on stage, a custom that has been followed since the first centuries of the Fujian puppet theatre when a performance had only two puppeteers.

Although manpower is no longer so limited, there is still the need for exactness and organization. A puppeteer must make quick changes. Often with a puppet on each hand, he will switch one without taking his eyes from the stage; or in other scenes, he will move a puppet from one hand to the other, without a break in pace, while reaching down for the next puppet.

Before a play begins, performers lay out their figures in a cloth pouch that is placed beneath the width of the stage. Every puppeteer arranges his own so that he is completely familiar with their placement and will have no doubts during a swift change of scene. Small pockets to the right and left of stage behind the curtain wings hold small props, such as swords, spears, fans, and pipes; these will be handed over at the appropriate moment by an assistant. As they are used, props and puppets are dropped noiselessly into the cloth pouch,

but they don't remain there for long. Almost immediately, apprentices or assistant puppeteers performing minor roles put them away, taking care with the puppets to fold the heads down and turn the costumes inside out to protect the embroidery and finely carved heads. Down through the centuries many legends warned that if puppets were not quickly removed from the stage after a performance and stored away in their cases (with heads packed

separately from the bodies), the figures would come to life and cause havoc.

Another backstage element which gives a polished look to a hand puppet performance is the dress of the puppeteers. The performers almost always wear long silken arm cuffs running the from wrist to above the elbow. Designed to decrease the visibility of the puppeteer's hands and wrists, these long cuffs are either color-matched to the puppet's costume or are solid black. The performer will also wear platform shoes if he is relatively short. Because he holds his puppet above his head and must perform at a set stage height, it is important that he be the correct height, or wear shoes with elevated soles to keep from straining. Of course, a puppeteer can also be too tall, and in that case, the performer must simply bend down during the show.

The backstage spectator may also be surprised to see men performing with a hairnet on, but this serves to press down unruly hair which would otherwise be visible above the level of the stage. It is concern for details such as these which makes the Fujian hand puppet performance so impressive.

Secrets of a Hand Puppet Performance

Besides special techniques, puppeteers have developed a number of backstage devices and concealed controls to enhance their performances. The puppeteer's term for these mechanisms, strings, or rods is *tong*, meaning "through," with the implication of being inside, or hidden. In hand puppetry controls or devices are never seen outside the figure, and this is in keeping with the beauty of this type of puppetry, which lacks distracting external rods

Newly designed heads for the film to be made of *The Eight Immortals Crossing the Ocean*, performed by the Longxi Region Hand Puppet Troupe.

or strings. For generations such performing mechanisms and devices were carefully guarded secrets in puppetry families. Many of the movements which fall in this category are among the simplest of human actions, but they become extraordinary when performed on stage by a puppet.

A number of such techniques are incorporated in one dramatic episode entitled *"Da-ming Prefecture,"* which is taken from the popular story cycle, *All Men Are Brothers* (*Shui-hu Zhuan*). The tale is much like that of Robin Hood, of righteous men who are forced to become outlaws when they refuse to bow to evil, traitorous officials. In this episode members of the rebel troupe sneak past the official in charge of the city gates by disguising themselves as itinerant acrobats and performers at the New Year's festival. This acrobatic tour de force is really a play within a play, as one sees rebels cleverly disguised as acrobats, jugglers, archers, lion dancers, baton masters, and plate spinners.

The comic focus of the scene is the gatekeeper, a pompous official who dominates his underlings yet cringes instantly when faced by a real adversary. He is a figure of unrelenting satire, and his long gown with its mandarin square emblematic of rank lends him no dignity. The wings of his hat vibrate constantly, and his head bobs up and down as he walks cockily to his official chair in front of the city gate. In his hand he carries a delicate fan which he waves back and forth in a constant motion. This movement is achieved by an internal bamboo rod running from the hand of the puppet through the figure's sleeve and costume, where it is moved by the puppeteer.

At the same time, the puppeteer has control of the gatekeeper's hat by means of a nylon string through the puppet's head and body. The wire is attached to a plastic loop which the puppeteer clamps in his teeth, as both his hands are now occupied. When he loosens the tension on the wire, the puppet's hat rides freely on his head, and by a deft twist it can be made to spin around the figure's head. After this humorous maneuver, the puppeteer re-tightens tension and the hat returns to its normal position. Later he will release the ring completely, allowing the hat to fall in such a way that the puppet can snatch it up in his hands. This action, too, always provokes much laughter.

In the same episode the gatekeeper reveals his luxurious habits as he smokes a pipe and then drinks wine—simple actions in themselves, but spellbinding in a puppet play. The puppet smokes his pipe by means of a tiny tube inserted inside the costume and running up to his mouth. Backstage an assistant performer lights a cigarette, inhales the smoke, and at the required time moves on stage to blow the smoke up the hidden tube. The gatekeeper, meanwhile, has raised a tiny pipe to his lips and then pulls it away to emit a cloud of smoke.

Drinking is a less complicated maneuver. A puppet on stage grasps a tiny wine pot containing water and spills some to prove to the audience that there really is liquid inside. Then the gatekeeper is passed a goblet, into which is poured a stream of "wine." After this the gatekeeper raises the goblet and drinks. In fact, however, there is nothing for him to drink because a wad of absorbent cotton in the bottom of the goblet has soaked up the water. Internal strings are used to control the puppets' hands, opening and closing to grasp or pass objects as necessary. This appears to be an easy sequence of movements, but it still requires superb coordination for the puppeteers to be able to grasp, hold, and exchange props using the tiny hands of their puppets.

Regional Differences

Two schools of hand puppetry developed in Fujian Province over the centuries as the popularity of this type of performance increased. Although these schools are termed northern and southern, their names derive not from regions, but from the type of music and singing they employ.

The northern school (or *bei-pai*), centering around the city of Zhangzhou, is actually located to the south. However, it incorporated the northern melodies and songs of Beijing and Hubei opera and the music known as *Yiyang qiang*, which developed in Yiyang County, Jiangxi Province during the sixteenth century. The music is sharp and fast-paced and emphasizes percussion instruments such as clappers, cymbal, gong, and drum. Traditionally, the repertoire of the northern school was composed primarily of operas with military themes which were performed in Beijing opera style.

The southern school, or *nan-pai*, is concentrated around Quanzhou and is characterized by the soft and poignant music of the south, which is relatively slow-paced and distinguished by flute and wind instruments. It is interesting that the string puppet theatre was a major influence upon the development of southern musical styles. It incorporated elements of the distinctively slow and soft type of music known as *kui-lei diao*, or "marionette melody," which was used in the string puppet theatre of Quanzhou.

In the twentieth century performers such as Yang Sheng began to attempt a consolidation of the finest performing aspects of both northern and southern schools. After 1949 the

Orchestra of the Longxi Hand Puppet Troupe.

new government encouraged cooperation between the two schools, and selected master performers of both types to perform together in important international competitions.

Over the centuries North China has also had its long tradition of one-man or small itinerant hand puppet troupes. This type of hand puppet theatre was called *li-zi xi* ("standing theatre") or *bian-dan xi* ("shoulder pole theatre"). The stage was a relatively simple affair that rested on the puppeteer's shoulders. It had long cloth drapes to conceal the body of the puppeteer, a tent-like roof and complete outer framework of a building in miniature. As there was usually only one performer, he would use his feet to strike drums and gongs

during the show and delivered all songs and speeches. The performer also used a whistle to provide accompaniment or to vary his voice to imitate animals, babies, or create other effects. Performances were necessarily limited to short, simple scenes; nevertheless, this was robust and rough folk theatre full of comedy and satire. A number of the popular pieces centered around heroes who subdued a tiger barehandedly. These itinerant performers were probably most active during the weeks of celebration during the lunar New Year. Performances grew fewer under the bitter economic conditions of the later nineteenth and early twentieth centuries, and today the form has disappeared entirely.

Training of a Hand Puppeteer

In the early days it was a bitter struggle for a young, would-be apprentice to find a master and complete an arduous apprenticeship. The traditional training period was set at three years and four months, and during this time, a student was the chattel of his master, subject to every tyranny the master might choose to exercise. In addition to the difficult training process itself, the apprentice was responsible for performing all sorts of daily chores and menial tasks that needed to be done. When a student finally reached a level at which he might begin performing, his wages were paid directly to his master. But it would be wrong to single out the acting profession for an excessively harsh apprentice system, as this was the traditional training process for any art, craft, or trade throughout Asia, and the practices of the puppetry world can have been no more difficult or stringent than those in other occupations. And if the training was severe, it was nevertheless effective, fostering the discipline and concern for perfection which assured mature performers astonishing success on the stage.

Something of the life of a student in the old system can be glimpsed in the story of the master hand puppeteer Yang Sheng of Fujian. As a boy of four, Yang Sheng had already begun to show a love of the art, carving puppets from sweet potatoes and using a wooden bench as his stage to give performances for his playmates. Since he was of a family traditionally engaged in puppetry, his father recognized his talent and took the boy along with him in his travels as a performer. Thus was his training initiated at the age of seven. His abilities were startling for one so young and the local people called him "the child master." At the age of fourteen he was acknowledged to be a full-fledged performer and was invited to join a troupe as the chief master performer.

In those days no puppeteer would reveal specialties or performing secrets: this was the only way to safeguard one's livelihood and a full rice bowl in a competitive society. It was a custom at that time for a rich patron to subsidize competitions between two troupes side-by-side, with the one drawing the largest audience declared to be the winner. Yang Sheng's troupe was called to represent the northern branch of hand puppetry in Fujian in a competition with the southern branch. Night after night the puppeteers performed, calling all their secret techniques into play. Yang Sheng, then only fourteen, represented his troupe for the first time in such a competition. He was young and had not yet attained his full strength, and eventually his voice began to fade from strain. One by one the audience eb-bed to the other stage until those who were left began to hiss and boo at Yang's performance. Angry and exhausted, he finally collapsed on stage after spitting out a mouthful of blood.

At that time there was no greater humiliation than for a northern branch representative to lose to one of the southern competitors, and this bitter defeat spurred Yang Sheng to work harder and harder. He quit his troupe intent on

learning the southern style of performance, but no one would teach him because he was not only from a competing troupe but from a competing school. Eventually he began to follow a southern troupe from place to place, carefully observing their performances every day from the audience. He became friends with the troupe members, but they would never discuss work with him. The main artist of this troupe was an old veteran with many years of stage exprience, but he had no family of his own. Yang Sheng began to help the master with chores and eventually the veteran taught him some of his simpler tricks, but none of the important ones. Sometime later, after Yang Sheng had gone away, he heard that this

Students rehearse the traditional opera *Da-Ming Prefecture* ; by gripping a wire between his teeth, the performer controls the movements of his puppet's fan.

Yang Feng in performance.

old master was very ill, and so the young puppeteer came to stay and care for his senior, buying him medicine and making him comfortable. The old puppeteer was dying and because he knew of Yang Sheng's sincerity and dedication to his art, he revealed his greatest secrets on his deathbed. That is how Yang Sheng came to master the abilities of both great puppetry traditions, selecting their finest elements to create a more perfect style of performance. He also studied the techniques of China's finest opera performers—Mei Lanfang and Zhou Xinfang—to incorporate elements of their technique into his repertoire.

In his teaching Yang Sheng had a motto: "If the jade is not ground, it cannot be made into a vessel." He was strict and demanding with his students, but he never hid his secrets from them. His goal was to spur them to excellence. Every morning it was his practice to have a pot of strong, dark tea and then instruct his students in their practice exercises. Sometimes an old stomach problem would recur, causing him to break out in sweat from the pain. But, rather than stop, he would merely grip his stomach with his hand and continue with the lesson.

Yang Sheng's son, Yang Feng, followed in his father's footsteps, becoming the fifth generation in the Yang family to study puppetry. At the age of twelve Yang Feng was already pushing himself in his craft, often practicing until his arms throbbed and his hands were numb. When he lifted his chopsticks to eat, his hands would shake from exhaustion. Yang Sheng saw this and ached for his son, but knew that skill was only attained through such suffering. "Now you have a formal school and proper teachers, full stomachs and scholarships to support your study," he said. "You do not have to worry about where your next bowl of rice will come from."

Yang Feng described his training under the stern tutelage of his father. As part of his practice exercises on early mornings in deep winter, his father had him plunge his hands into a barrel of freezing cold water until his hands felt frozen stiff and his body shivered with cold. This way, even if the young puppeteer had the inclination to be lazy, he would still be forced to be energetic just to warm up his body. After one or two hours, his father would come out to inspect his hands: only if his palms were warm to the touch did this show that he had been practising hard enough. If not then his father would hit him. Yang Feng finished this story by saying to his children with deep emotion: "If not for your grandfather's severe training methods, how would I have earned the artistic skill I have today?"

Today's puppeteer enters a very different world of training, one with a broader, more formal and more regularized process of study. Modern students begin study around the age

42

of fourteen or fifteen and attend professional puppetry schools which teach a basic three-year core of performance subjects as well as other general requirements such as language, mathematics, and science. Students also take courses in related arts such as painting, sculpture, and music appreciation. To ensure a strong background they must also learn costuming, design, and carving of puppet heads. For special subjects they may go to other schools for short-term training as necessary, and on occasion the school will even invite outside teachers in to give training in special areas of performance. In addition to these subjects the young hand puppeteer must also study local opera, learning its music, songs, and movement, since all of these elements are adapted

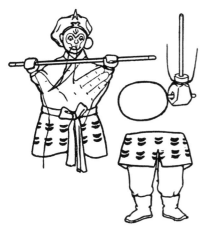

on a finer scale to the puppet theatre. Although this breadth of study might seem strange to us, it reflects the traditionally close connection between the human opera and the puppet theatre in China and the serious training required of the would-be puppeteer.

The key to excellence lies in mastery of positions and movements and in absolute control of the hands. A hand puppeteer's hands are a thing of beauty, with the expressiveness and purity of line of a ballet dancer's body. He is taught the close correspondence between the structure of the hand and the body: just as the arm has three jointed sections (upper arm to elbow, elbow to wrist, and hand), so does the hand. Bending the wrist makes the puppet bow at the waist, as the top of the palm becomes the puppet's chest. The hand puppeteer must learn to control the movement of each finger joint to reproduce the motion of the arm. The forefinger acts as the spine of the puppet, holding it erect and serving as a pivot.

The question is how to progress from moving the hand and fingers to creating a human figure. The hand puppetry school of Fujian develops this skill in three stages. First, students learn the basic finger and hand positions, just as a ballet dancer must first learn the five basic postures. In classical hand puppetry, there are five frequently used hand positions.

The second step in training is to learn to coordinate these separate positions into a sequence of movements to represent important actions such as walking, running, dancing and so forth. The puppeteer must learn to combine a number of elements to create a realistic effect. Movements are concurrent; in walking, the head juts forward while arms swing back and forth. There are some thirty pattern movements which must be learned, of which about ten or so are frequently used in performance. These practice exercises, called *lian-gong*, form an essential part of every puppeteer's daily schedule. The first months of training are especially important because proper patterns must

The placement of the hand inside the puppet of Monkey, as well as Monkey's hand and lower body part.

Controlling two hand
puppets simultaneously
in a fight scene.

be established at this time, and thus students get much personal supervision at the beginning of study. It is also essential in the early months of training to develop the shoulder and arm strength which will permit hand puppeteers to perform for long hours in the taxing position requisite of their profession—with arms fully extended overhead.

The third step of basic training is to master the complex maneuvers and acrobatics of martial arts and battle scenes, known as *wu-gong*. These three stages of training form the basis of the first three years of a puppeteer's study. Then come two more years of advanced training which are also divided into three stages. First, students learn the conventions and formulaic movements of human opera by studying the Beijing or a local opera, and then how to apply these to the puppet theatre. Man and puppet should become fused in this process, and to encourage this unity, students are taught to move with the same defined gait and precise stance as their puppets.

Next the young puppeteers begin to learn *xue-xi*, or teaching operas, which include the essential movements and dramatic elements of the puppet theatre. At this point the student chooses the category of character in which he or she will specialize in later years. In spite of their specialization, the puppeteers must also learn the basics of all the other character types—be they comic, martial, or feminine—so that they have a complete mastery of this dramatic form.

After this the young puppeteer begins to tackle the harder classical operas in the repertory of his troupe. There are presently 319 full-length operas in the repertory of the Longxi Hand Puppet Troupe, for example. Later on,

they may create their own operas, but only after they have thoroughly mastered the classics. Tradition always comes first; only after acquiring a disciplined technique and mature dramatic skills does a performer earn the license for creativity.

The program of the Longxi Region Hand Puppetry School reflects the careful, detailed training provided for professional puppeteers in China today. There are twenty-seven students in the school and six full-time instructors. Four teach performing skills, one teaches carving, and one teaches percussion instruments—especially gong and drum, which set the rhythm for a performance. There are close family connections between students and teachers and troupe members, with several family members often involved in different aspects of the art. Such close rapport between the performers creates a true living tradition: performers steeped in a centuries-old art, integrating it into their lives to a degree difficult to comprehend in the West.

44

Longxi has only one professional troupe, but there are twenty-four spare-time or amateur troupes in the area. Such amateur performers learn from friends or family members, or from special short-term courses given occasionally by the regional puppetry school. The government today encourages these amateur performers but provides no economic support; ticket sales are their only source of income. And yet, under the present policy of increased economic flexibility, amateur entertainments are expected to continue to multiply.

Rural areas are the biggest supporters of traditional puppet operas, given by both amateur and professional troupes. In keeping with the government policy of "serving the people," professional troupes are required to go to the countryside every year to perform, often under difficult conditions. Troupes organized at the city level must spend four months yearly performing in the countryside, while national-level troupes, like the Longxi Hand Puppet Troupe, must set aside two months. Thus puppet plays are enjoyed throughout the country.

中国木偶艺术

The soul of the marionette is born of the puppeteer's skill in handling the strings. In its master's hands, it can express an extraordinary range of motions and emotions, captivating an audience with its grace, elegance, and fluid pacing.

Marionettes have been traced far back in China, and it is likely that the earliest puppet figure discovered in China was, in fact, a string puppet. By the Tang dynasty the marionette theatre was very well developed and was capable of highly sophisticated movements. The eighth-century Tang emperor Xuan-zong, as an example of the extent of influence this art had upon the contemporary imagination, compared human existence to the controlled performance of a marionette in one of his poems.

More than any other form of Chinese puppetry, marionette theatre retains elements of ritual and spiritual observances. The belief in its ability to influence the spirit world came from Chinese folk religion, which pictured the world as crowded with spirits ready to do good or evil as the mood took them, and unfortunately for the vulnerable humans around them, their mood was usually toward the latter. These ghostly forces were quick to inhabit any object open to their possession, and puppets, having human shape, were especially desirable. For that reason puppets were always kept locked in a stage case, with the heads stored separately from the bodies.

Chinese histories from the Ming and Qing dynasties record cases in which old puppets

STRING PUPPETS 4

created havoc, dancing under the full moon and whispering as if in a performance. These old puppets were said to come from old discarded cases which had been long forgotten, and having no master puppeteer to control them, they took on a life of their own. The Chinese believed that anything extremely old acquired its own special powers and was subject to possession by spirits. This phenomenon was recorded in a fourth century alchemical and religious work:

The spirits in old objects...are capable of assuming human shape for the purpose of confusing human vision and constantly putting human beings to a test. It is only when reflected in a mirror that they are unable to alter their true forms. (Ware, p. 281)

Only a master puppeteer trained in the charms and amulets of folk Taoism was thought capable of controlling the old puppets. By using special incantations and charms the puppeteer could invoke a good deity to inhabit the puppet and cause it to expel evil ghosts in the area.

In many parts of China this heritage of folk religion and superstition was preserved by puppetry well into the twentieth century, especially in the southeastern provinces of Guangdong and Fujian. There, ritual was a curious amalgam of ancient terms and amulets from folk Taoism, of sympathetic magic, and religious plays influenced by Buddhism and folklore. Plays portraying a hero overcoming a tiger were held to be especially efficacious for exorcisms. Although such practices have been banned in China since 1949, recently in Hong Kong, a theatre built in an inauspicious location was plagued by apparitions and required the services of a puppet troupe to expel the bad

spirits. A ritual play was performed and as it began, the doors of the theatre flung open by themselves, indicating that the ghosts had been frightened away by the power of the performance. *(Pimpaneau, p.22)*

The "Theatre of Auspicious Rituals"

Located on a magnificent bay where the Jin River empties into the East China Sea, Quanzhou is none other than the fabulous Zayton from which Marco Polo departed on his return journey to Venice. Over nine hundred years ago, Syrian and Southeast Asian merchants landed here and unloaded holds full of pearls, spices, and rare woods before laying in the tea, silks, and porcelain for which the region is famed. Marco Polo described the harbor's bustle and rich trade in those days:

The noble and handsome city of Zayton, which has a port on the seacoast celebrated for the resort of shipping, loaded with merchandise, that is afterwards distributed through every part of (southeast China)...It is indeed impossible to convey an idea of the number of merchants and the accumulation of goods in this place, which is held to be one of the largest ports in the world. (Komroff, pp. 254-5)

Marco Polo visited Quanzhou at its height, bustling with foreign merchants and sailors, pilgrims, and missionaries. Even in the tenth century, the city was estimated to have had 500,000 inhabitants, whose numbers were swelled by the many foreign merchants and priests living in the city. Islam, Nestorianism, Manichaeism, Judaism, and Hinduism were among the foreign religions found in

Quanzhou even before the early arrival of the traveller Marco Polo.

The name Zayton—in one of those unpredictable tricks of linguistic exchange—is now a permanent entry in the English lexicon: "satin" was the lustrous, thick silk made in the region and exported from this port in great quantities.

The city today appears not to have changed much since the middle ages. Narrow, teeming streets curve past one- and two-story brick row houses and open-fronted stores, where residents gather to talk and buy. Since the time of Marco Polo, an ancient stone bridge with huge stone slabs laid across stone pillars spans the Luoyang River where it enters the sea, and the great Mosque with its massive stone gate still towers above Tumen Street.

It has long been the custom in southeastern Fujian and Quanzhou to arrange for string puppet performances to propitiate the spirits and expel malevolent forces at events such as weddings, birthdays, completion of a new building, or after fires, disasters, or deaths. Called the *jia-li xi* or "theatre of auspicious rituals," the Quanzhou marionette theatre was probably brought to the south as early as the tenth century with the large migrations of people fleeing the chaotic invasions in northern China. The dialogue portion of the Quanzhou string puppet theatre is, in fact, called "the speech of the central regions." The music, songs, and diction of this theatre are extremely old and reflect the cultural conservatism of this region.

This type of theatre is also unique in the high status accorded its performers in feudal society. Puppeteers of the *jia-li* theatre could sit for the civil service examinations, while other performers and actors—along with criminals, slaves, and prostitutes—were barred from taking the examinations under the Confucian belief that they were riffraff. String puppeteers wore the long gown and ceremonial hat of scholars. If other troupes passed a *jia-li* troupe in the area or on the road, custom required that

One of the Twin Pagodas of Quanzhou's Kai-yuan Temple.

they send a member over to pay respects to the patron deity of the *jia-li* theatre called *Xiang-gong Ye* (meaning, roughly, the Old Lord Minister). In addition, their performances could not begin until after the string puppet performance had started.

As part of the spiritual power of the *jia-li* theatre, a strict ritual was observed preceding every performance. First a troupe member backstage struck a large gong three times, then a drum once. Then, after checking that everything was in readiness for the performance, he would strike the drum a second time, followed by the bell-shaped gong. When the drum was struck for the third time, a performer went before the patron deity and burned incense, laying out an offering of wine and lighting paper tinsel. The whole troupe would chant a three-word spell to drive away evil and bring harmony, and a representation of the deity was brought from its place outside the stage tent and hung up on the central pole behind the stage. This was followed by another chant, called the "10,000-year joy," to invoke the deity to come down and inhabit his puppet image. The puppet would perform a ritual dance to purify the stage, accompanied by the auspicious chants of the other troupe members, and having "trod the stage," he was again hung up on the central pole directly behind the stage, and the regular performance began. The performance was not considered officially over until the deity was brought back on stage to bid farewell.

This example of ritual demonstrates the connection between puppetry and folk religion in the popular Chinese imagination. Because of the preeminence of the Quanzhou style of

string puppets, not only in the past but in modern China as well, it is the focus of our look at Chinese string puppetry.

The traditional Quanzhou marionette stage was about three feet high and seven feet square, with a curtain hung across the bottom of the stage. Behind the curtain were hung the play texts. About midway back from the front of the stage a screen was arranged to conceal the puppeteers, who performed standing at the rear of the stage. Before 1949 troupes had four performers portraying the four categories of roles: *sheng* or males; *dan* or females; *bei*, roughly equivalent to the *jing* or painted face roles of northern drama; and *za* which were miscellaneous character types. Most troupes had about thirty-six puppets which could represent all the personalities of their plays.

There were four musicians in each troupe: one to play the large and small drums; one to play the *suo-na*; one to strike the bell-shaped gong and play the vertical bamboo flute; and one to play the small gong, large drum, and copper cymbal. The music of the string theatre is a soft southern style of melody developed especially for the marionette theatre and called *kuilei-diao* (puppet music). It has a rather slow but clear rhythm, and up to now more than four hundred of its different melodies have been transcribed for posterity.

Control and Basic Movements

Traditional marionettes required at least eight strings for control of head, body, feet, and arms, but there was no set rule as to the number or disposition of the strings. More could be added as occasioned by actions of a play and as permitted by the ability of the puppeteer. Before modern innovations, the number of strings per figure never exceeded twenty and they averaged four feet in length.

Puppets today are considerably more complex and demanding. The number of strings per marionette has been increased to as many as thirty-two, but sixteen is the average. They are arranged as follows:

Head: two, which do not move, but simply hold the puppet upright

Back: one, through the back to nod and turn the head
  Chest: one
  Feet: one each
  Knees: one each
  Wrists: one each
  Hands: one for each four-finger unit
  Arms: one for each lower arm, and one for each elbow

String figure of a general, one of the puppets in the collection of the Quanzhou Marionette troupe.

51

Design of a Quanzhou Marionette with the traditional control.

The hands and feet of the Quanzhou marionette are very important in recognizing a puppet's character type. Feet are of three kinds—bare, women's, and booted. Hands are either civil (*wen*) or martial (*wu*). The former are carved in two separate sections of thumb and four fingers so that they can be drawn together by strings to grasp objects such as brushes, fans, pipes, cups, and so forth. The hands of military characters are carved into a fist, into which weapons can be inserted for fight scenes. Other strings are added to render special movements, such as a thumb string which opposes thumb and fingers so that objects can be grasped; a string to bring the arms together; and calf strings to lift the feet in a natural backward walk. Another innovation is the addition of a string inside the sleeve to straighten out the arm and create an impression of strength and forceful movement. The increase in strings has meant that today one person cannot always control one puppet. For an important character who wields many props such as Sun Wukong, the Monkey King, two puppeteers must work together to execute his complicated movements.

Marionettes are manipulated through use of a wooden control which secures the path of the strings. Most controls are constructed in a cross, T-bar, or "I" shape, or in a rectangle connected to a handle. While performing, the puppeteer holds the handle with thumb and forefinger, shifting the control to execute head movements and major body movements. Using the middle, ring, and forefingers of one hand to direct the path of the strings, the puppeteer uses his other hand to perform all string movements, of which there are essentially only four: pulling in, pushing away, moving to the side, and raising up.

The most striking change in the modern Quanzhou marionette theatre, however, has come with the adoption of a higher stage divided into three parallel playing areas which create the illusion of near, middle, and distant perspective when coupled with the use of large and small puppets. The three stages also allow an effective combination of marionettes with hand and rod puppets. Over the main stage, a metal walkway called the "sky bridge" is the center from which performers manipulate the fifteen-foot long marionette strings, while hand and rod puppets are operated from below next to the platform called the "earth stage." The marionette remains the heart of the performance, while other types of puppets are used judiciously for special effects. Hand puppets, because they follow the shape of the palm and lack strings, are more easily manipulated in martial art and acrobatic scenes; rod puppets are used for dances, certain fighting sequences, and to depict moving objects such as butterflies or darting goldfish. In the traditional play, *Mountain of Fire*, eight different puppets of various sizes and types are employed to portray the main character, the irrepressible and incorrigible Monkey King, as he ranges over the three playing areas.

The Quanzhou marionette theatre has developed a strict system of rules governing performance. One of the first basic rules is that when the marionettist is performing on the right side of the stage he must hold the control with his right hand and vice versa. This practice ensures that the control and strings, when held suspended, will not block the view of

Monkey urges the White Dragon Horse on towards the Mountain of Fire.

other performers. As a puppeteer moves his figure across the stage, he or she must shift the control from one hand to the other, a maneuver which can result in an abrupt slackness of the strings if the performer is not extremely quick and dexterous. The fluid exchange of the control between hands is an important basic performing skill because even a momentary loss of control can destroy the illusion of life which a puppeteer works so hard to create.

The Chinese say that the skill of a marionettist is most clearly displayed in the walk of the puppet. This most basic of human movements requires fluid coordination of legs, feet, and arms for a realistic look. To create this motion, the puppeteer keeps the head and shoulder strings taut, raising and lowering the knee strings in turn with one hand and using the control in the other hand to make the body sway lightly from side to side. A slightly more complicated walk adds movement of one or both arms through manipulation of the lower arm string. A walk is very expressive, a clue to the character's personality. Female characters have a slow, fluid gait with a gentle sway; military figures have a forceful, abrupt pace; officials walk with a slow, deliberate step suggesting thoughtfulness and dignity, while the walk of comic characters may contain all sorts of eccentric or peculiar elements.

In exploring ways to give more stability to the marionette, contemporary puppeteers have added to their traditional techniques the use of weights on the feet of the figure. Another innovation is to have an assistant stand under the playing area of the high stage, and from there anchor the marionette's feet when the character is not in motion. In this way the puppeteer can execute strong, abrupt poses without causing the figure's feet and body to sway or shift.

It is hard to deny the almost mystical power of a puppet performance to transport one into an ancient world of magnificent heroes and grand villains. Wearing miniature gowns of crimson, black, or turquoise silk, hand-embroidered in traditional designs, the marionettes prance and spin, stride or stagger across a stage that seems to expand with their every step. After witnessing their subtlety and economy of motion, one finds human performers of Chinese opera clumsy and overblown, curiously gross and excessive in gesture.

Generations of master craftsmen in Quanzhou have analyzed the components of costume, structure, carving and painting in order to maximize the dramatic effect of these elements. Costumes, for example, rely upon disproportionately long trailing sleeves and lengthened skirts to dramatize each movement, while elaborate and colorful hair or headdresses elongate a puppet's two-foot frame and draw attention to the expressive face. And the faces are crucial to the effectiveness of the marionette. Designs painted on the face immediately identify a character and its personality type. In addition, puppet carvers will extend the brow ridge and enlarge the eyes to focus attention on a puppet's expression, be it fierce and angry or gentle and shy. Extra refinements come with the addition of movable earlobes, hinged jaws, or eyes which close and open. Finally, the head size has been increased in recent years in order to command greater attention and make the miniature performers more visible when playing to large audiences.

All of these dramatic elements come into play to create the elegant Quanzhou style. Known for its soft music, the theatre has a fluency enhanced by expressive dance movements. The traditional repertoire was composed of *wen* or civil plays, but special techniques had to be developed to portray fighting scenes. Unlike the forceful, staccato movements of a hand puppet battle scene, marionettes are more graceful and deliberate in their pace. Figures do not strike one another, but come together, cross weapons, and then draw apart. In recent years innovations such as anchoring the feet and using a sleeve string to extend the arm for thrusts have added to the forcefulness of movement, but the overall softness of the performance has been preserved.

Backstage Preparations

In earlier years the most important of backstage preparations involved the placement of the theatre's patron deity. There were two forms of the deity's image: one was a marionette used in the pre-performance ritual and then hung directly behind the stage to receive offerings. In the stomach of this marionette were hidden a scissor, a traditional carpenter's measure, a copper mirror, and kernels of the five kinds of grains, all of which were emblems of the deity's powers. The other form of the patron deity was carved of wood or clay and was flanked on the left by a golden rooster and to the right by a jade dog. This triad was worshipped in the theatre or in the home of the head performer; it was never taken outside.

A traditional hand puppet stage with elaborate wood carving and gilt decoration, from the Lutz Collection, University of Richmond.

The Immortal Maidens come to the Garden of Peaches of Immortality to pick fruit for the Queen Mother's great festival.

Monkey confronts the Guardian of the Banana Leaf Fan and her husband, the Cow Devil King, in the episode *Mountain of Fire* performed by the Quanzhou Marionette Troupe.

Two young scholars, rod puppets from northeastern China. (Collection of Alan G. Cook; photo by Mary Carolyn Pindar)

Two embroiderers who specialize in making costumes for the Longxi Region Hand Puppet Troupe. Costume is first embroidered in one piece, then cut and sewn into final shape.

Two rod puppets used in performance of China Art Puppet Troupe.

Military commander with elaborate headdress and hands carved to hold weapons. *(Collection of Nancy Lohman Staub; photo by Mary Carolyn Pindar)*

Center is Cao Cao, the wily and ruthless prime minister at the end of the failing Han Dynasty.

Fifth-generation master puppeteer Yang Feng demonstrates the movements of a warrior.

Close-up look at a scene from *Eight Immortals Cross the Ocean.*

Mounted General wearing armor and commander's headdress. *(Collection of Professor and Mrs. Derk Bodde; photo by Mary Carolyn Pindar)*

The setting up of the stage and placement of the patron deity were handled by non-performing assistants who also handled the stage cases. After these preliminaries, the puppeteers dressed the marionettes and added hats, turbans, and inserted the weapons or special props to be used in the performance. There were traditionally thirty-six categories of characters, and the marionettes of each category had a set position where they were hung in the wings before the performance. Hats and reserve puppet heads were placed to the right and left of the stage, and the bag containing spears and swords was hung on the pole at the front right corner of the stage. Play texts were suspended on a horizontal beam above the stage.

Today there is still a set location where each marionette is hung before a performance, generally according to the order of appearance. At this time each string is carefully checked to be sure that none is loose, tangled, or broken.

In earlier years it was a common backstage trick to hang less important puppets on a nail at the rear of the stage during periods when they were not required to move. Because the troupe was small, with only four or five puppeteers, this permitted more characters to be involved. In some cases performers even hung secondary marionettes on their chests or upper arms, while simultaneously operating a marionette in each hand. The technique is no longer necessary because stage size and troupe members have been increased. Today, in fact, the trend is to create more and more complicated and detailed actions which can require two or sometimes even three performers per puppet.

After a marionette is no longer needed on stage, it is immediately whisked backstage.

Cast of characters for *Flooding Gold Mountain Temple.*

Holding the strings together with one hand and grasping the control with the other, the marionettist gives a quick spin and the figure is wound into a tight twist. This keeps the lines from getting tangled or broken—a particular concern when one is working with marionettes for the high stage having fifteen-foot strings!

Secrets of Marionette Performance

One of the most popular pieces in the Quanzhou repertoire, called *Shui Man Jin-shan* (*Flooding Gold Mountain Temple*), combines all of the dramatic elements of the Quanzhou style. This play is based upon the legendary tale of Lady White Snake which probably dates back to the Tang dynasty and has appeared since in

Little Blue, a valiant woman warrior and faithful companion to Lady White Snake in puppet play of that title. *(Collection of the Quanzhou Marionette Troupe; photo by Mary Carolyn Pindar)*

a number of different adaptations as short stories and plays. The modern version of the legend, called *Bai-she Zhuan* (*The Tale of the White Snake*), was completed in 1953 by the well known playwright Tian Han. The piece centers around the ill-fated love of a serpent spirit Lady White who takes on human form and comes to visit Hangzhou with her faithful companion Little Blue, also a transformed snake spirit. Lady White falls in love with a young scholar Xu Xian. They marry and soon are expecting a child. Their happy union is disturbed, however, by the interference of Fa Hai ("Ocean of the Law"), the Abbot of Gold Mountain Temple, who knows the true origins of Lady White, and seeks to take Xu Xian from her and convert him to Buddhism.

One of the highlights of the Quanzhou marionette performance is their deft use of gesture and details to delineate the characters. Fa Hai, for example, languidly waves a yak tail whisk emblematic of his power and stamps his foot in anger when his plans are thwarted. He never directly faces anyone, but prefers to stare arrogantly over their heads as a sign that his piety is only an outward display. One of his young novice monks, meanwhile, is constantly scratching his body in a comically vulgar manner, rubbing his buttocks and waving his monk's cap. The total effect is of anything but piety. Xu Xian appears beset by emotion as he stamps his foot and beats his breast in anger, spins his long queue around his head in terror, or rubs away his tears with the trailing sleeve of his gown. His weakness of character and inability to discern people's true natures emerge clearly through these gestures. Little Blue, on the other hand, shows her honesty and directness as she draws and waves her sword at the slightest hint of treachery and rushes off to battle with no thought for her own safety. She is bold, impertinent, and somewhat hot-blooded—a true folk heroine.

One of the funniest and most inventive moments of the performance is the appearance of the water creatures which come to the aid of Lady White. One by one these allies float

64

above the waves of the river, showing first their natural marine form and then momentarily revealing an anthropomorphic aspect. Human arms, legs, neck, and head dart forth from a turtle's shell, for example. At a strategic moment, the turtle's neck grows and his head pivots comically. The crowning touch is the official's cap on his head—a perfect display of folk impertinence because Chinese folklore holds that the turtle is an immoral creature whose offspring can never be sure of their parentage due to the unusual way in which the eggs are fertilized. Next a clam shell opens to reveal a small boy within, and inside the brittle shell of a crayfish is a peculiar little figure with a protuberant forehead. By letting the audience in on the concealment, the puppeteers draw sympathy to the crustacean troops as they go to battle against the forces of Fa Hai. These warriors pose menacingly, but when their backs are turned, the hidden weapons of the water creatures flash out and land several sharp blows before disappearing again.

Traditional puppet shows, like the human theatre, lacked scenery or backdrops; even props were held to the barest minimum. In recent years, new forms of scenery have been devised and the White Snake episode incorporates a particularly attractive one. Painted on silk in muted aqua and red pastels, the subtle brushwork of the backdrop reflects both the influence of traditional Chinese landscape painting and the more realistic painting style of the West. The result is a totally effective blend of old and new.

Another play that clearly demonstrates the unique performing techniques of the Quanzhou Marionette Troupe is their *Huo-yan Shan* (*Mountain of Fire*). This is one episode

Lady White and Little Blue outside the temple walls.

Little Blue prepares to fight.

The young novice.

The Cow Devil King has
an evil plan.

Monkey confronts the evil
Guardian of the Banana
Leaf Fan.

Monkey in a magic
transformation.

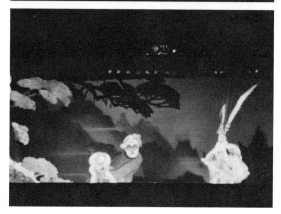

from the popular cycle of stories known as *Xi-you Ji* (*Journey to the West*). The episode was newly adapted in 1979 for performance with the high playing stage, and combines rod, hand, and string figures. By drawing upon the special capabilities of each style of puppetry and the three-dimensional effect of the high stage, the troupe has enhanced the dramatic appeal of its performance while preserving all the traditional flavor.

The story concerns the pilgrimage of the famous Buddhist monk Xuan-zang, who traveled to India in the seventh century to bring the sacred texts of Buddhism to China. According to historical records, in AD 627 Xuan-zang encountered a mountain of fire about twenty-five miles from Turpan, an oasis on the ancient caravan routes which skirted the treacherous Taklimakan desert.

The play presents a more fantastic version of this event, however. The monk is accompanied by the clever and resourceful Sun Wukong, the Monkey King. Also joining them is Zhu Bajie, or Pigsy, a corpulent and rather dull-witted creature too often at the mercy of his earthly appetites. Their adventures entail a number of spectacular effects, including a dazzling series of transformations between a character known as the Cow Devil King and the Monkey King. When the Cow Devil King becomes a bird, Monkey becomes an eagle; when the bird becomes a wolf, Monkey changes into a tiger. Finally the Cow Devil King transforms himself into a huge cow, but Monkey pulls out a handful of hairs and changes them into a score of little monkeys, who attack the cow. Thus the Cow Devil King is overcome and at last Monkey is able to extinguish the mountain of fire and can continue the journey to India with Pigsy and Xuan-zang.

This boisterous episode contains all the requisite elements of folk drama: earthy humor, fantasy, and anti-bureaucratic satire. The personalities are brought to life through deft elements of characterization and the superb technical skills of the performers. The main figure is undoubtedly Monkey, who quivers with barely restrained exuberance. His head turns from side to side, his nose twitches, and he seems always to be one step ahead of everyone else. Pigsy, in contrast, always seems to move more clumsily and think more slowly than the others. When he becomes excited or afraid, his large ears twitch violently. The Cow Devil King, on the other hand, appears rather pompous, while the monk floats in a spiritual cloud, unable to deal with any mundane problems which confront him. His motions are slow and controlled, in keeping with the characteristics of his persona.

One of the most exacting scenes occurs when the Cow Devil King hands Monkey a fan which Monkey grasps tightly. This difficult maneuver is executed by pulling Monkey's four fingers close to the palm through a special string added for this purpose. When marionettes are almost touching like this, strings can easily become entangled, especially longer strings. Each step must be carefully prearranged and each motion must be precise.

During the play, we see a number of variations in types of puppets. When hand puppets are used, the motion becomes very fast and is quite realistic. Another dimension is added when Monkey encounters an old sage who is, in fact, a human performer wearing a puppet-

Monkey fearlessly confronts his enemy.

like face mask. This actor stands on the lower stage and Monkey flies down from the high stage to stand on the sage's hand. At that moment, Monkey is represented by a special marionette made smaller than normal size to keep the proper ratio of size between the two figures in the scene.

Marionettes are used during a humorous scene with Pigsy. One performer stands on the high playing platform operating Pigsy's hands, while another stands below the lower stage, moving or anchoring his feet as necessary. At one point Pigsy falls down in an awkward sprawl, an action which can be achieved only through the cooperation of the two puppeteers above and below.

The success of the play and its broad range of movements is clearly dependent on the great variety of puppets in different sizes and styles. More than seventy puppets are necessary to portray the thirteen major and minor characters in the play. As mentioned above, eight different puppets are used for Monkey

67

alone. In a dazzling sequence of actions, Monkey, performed by a *small hand puppet*, swaggers, dances, and fights his way across the middle stage, then is thrown off into the air, and reemerges from the front stage as a *larger marionette*, only to disappear and reappear as a *tiny rod puppet* soaring off into the far distance. By progressing to smaller and smaller puppets, the puppeteers have learned to create the illusion of depth and distance within the confines of their small stage.

Regional Differences

The tradition of marionette performance lives on in other regions of China besides Quanzhou. The Longyan region of Western Fujian Province, for example, about 170 miles from Quanzhou, has a very well developed style of marionette theatre. Originally the marionettes had five strings, but later were expanded to ten, twelve, and sixteen strings. The puppets, made of braided bamboo strips, also increased in size from a little over one foot at the beginning to more than three feet.

This region practices two different methods of manipulation. With the first method, one puppeteer controls one puppet, holding the wooden control in his left hand while his right hand manipulates the strings, much as the Quanzhou puppeteers perform. However, for very fine movements, the puppeteer wears a special braided bamboo circle. The advantage of this method is that the performer can temporarily suspend the control from the top of this bamboo circle and thus free both hands to make delicate manipulations of the strings. This type of braided bamboo circle with its related techniques is unique to this area. With

the second method of manipulation, one puppeteer controls two puppets simultaneously, one in the left hand and one in the right. Sometimes even more puppets can be controlled by hanging the additional figures over the wrist, which may be done during fighting scenes. The puppeteer can manipulate even greater numbers of marionettes through the use of a "running horse circle," a larger loop on which four puppets can be suspended at one time. In this way a puppeteer holding one "running horse circle" in each hand can portray eight different figures at the same time. Although the movements in such an instance are of necessity rather limited, this technique is useful when a large group of characters must cross the stage together.

Stories about the origin of the western Fujian marionette theatre have been passed down locally for generations. It is said that in the early years of the Ming dynasty four men from the region traveled to Hangzhou and joined the marionette troupes there. After their apprenticeships were finished, they returned to Shanghang County in Fujian and organized its first marionette troupe. During the Guangxu period of the Qing dynasty (1875-1908), there was a great flowering of puppetry in Shanghang County, and more than one hundred professional troupes were performing plays at that time.

There are two different types of marionette troupes in western Fujian. The first type has three artists per troupe: two to manipulate the puppets and one to play the percussive instruments characteristic of this performance style.

During the performance one man leads the singing while the other two accompany him. The second type of troupe developed later and its main distinction is having four rather than two puppeteers.

The early troupes of the region had only eighteen types of puppet roles, and these eighteen character types were called the eighteen *Lohan* (Buddhist perfected being). Over the years this number expanded to twenty-four and finally to thirty-six.

The popular characters of this regional theatre are *sheng* (masculine leading role), *dan* (feminine leading role), *jing* (painted face), and *chou* (clown) of Beijing opera. Of these categories of roles, the *chou* has been the most important. Local legend equates the *chou* with the patron saint of the marionette theatre. After a performance when the costumes, props, and puppets were returned to their cases, *chou* marionettes were always placed on top so that they would not be pressed down by the other figures. Should they mistakenly be placed

The Quanzhou marionettes recreate the lion taming, ending with marionette dancers emerging from the lion.

lower in the case, the *chou* figures were said to climb up to the top of the case during the night. Such stories show that the *chou* character is held to possess particular power and vitality.

These troupes specialized in special formulaic gestures. For example, when a civil official came on stage, he would always make four gestures in his first appearance: straightening his official hat, patting his clothing, pulling up his robe, and holding his belt level with two hands. Male characters always walk in *ba-zi* or "eight character" steps, a measured gait with toes pointing outward, so named because the stance resembles the two slanting strokes of the Chinese character for eight. Female roles always take small steps and raise the foot only very slightly. The types of role are well established through such formulaic movements.

According to the old artists, this school had about one thousand plays in the traditional repertoire. Most were classical tales such as the *Tale of the White Snake, Journey to the West,* and *All Men Are Brothers.* The school is also well known for its portrayal of the episode, *Daming Fu,* which was described in the chapter on hand puppets. This style of marionettes continues to be popular today in the rural areas of western Fujian.

In the 1950s there were marionette troupes active in the Meixian and Longchuan districts of Guangdong Province, but they never achieved the complexity of technique which the Fujianese performers display, and it is likely that organized troupes in those areas disappeared after the vicissitudes of the Cultural Revolution. In 1956, however, the Longchuan Art Marionette Troupe was assigned to perform in the neighboring province of Guangxi

and has continued to be popular there. Its repertoire includes modernized versions of episodes from *Journey to the West* and *The White Snake*, as well as plays for children.

Up until the 1930s Shanghai had a number of popular string troupes which were often called to perform at guild festivities in the city. Their repertoire centered upon episodes from *Journey to the West*. Unfortunately, these troupes had disappeared in the city by the 1940s. After 1949, itinerant marionette troupes continued to be active in the rural regions of northeastern Jiangsu Province, performing for peasants in the villages. Their performances were rather basic and their figures had only seven to ten strings. Such troupes are no longer active today. In the early part of the twentieth century the cities of Nanjing and Beijing also had a few marionette troupes, but neither city has one today.

String puppets have been popular in North China since the eighth century. In the provinces of Shanxi and Shaanxi, the rather simple, small-scale marionette troupes loved by the peasants have continued to perform in the countryside to this day.

中国木偶艺术

From north to south and east to west, a visitor to almost any province in China today would discover some form of rod puppet theatre being performed. The most widespread form of puppets in the country, rod puppets have been used to develop something of a national style of puppet performance, as exemplified by state-level troupes in Beijing and Shanghai. These troupes have concentrated on modernizing their performances with new types of lighting, special effects, and Western-influenced music and plays, which unfortunately, has meant at the sacrifice of some traditional flavor.

The general term for rod puppets in China is *zhang-tou mu-ou*, or *zhang-tou kui-lei* ("staff-head puppet") which was a term in use by the Song dynasty. It is probable that rod puppets had appeared even earlier and that they formed the basis of the comic slapstick pieces centering around the character Bald Guo which were well known in the sixth century. Other terms for the rod theatre are *shou-tuo xi* or *tuo xi*, meaning "hand-supported theatre" and "palm-supported theatre," derived from the way in which the puppets are maneuvered. Another term is *gun-ju mu-ou*, meaning "rod-held puppets." As we shall see, however, rod puppets are not at all uniform; they acquired distinctive features as they spread to different regions, and different names as well.

Members of the Shanghai Puppet Troupe demonstrate roles from *The Ruby*.

ROD PUPPETS 5

Special Features of the Rod Puppet

The many different types of rod puppets in China may be roughly divided into three categories by size. Most are larger than hand puppets or shadow figures which makes them ideal for large audiences. The control mechanisms can also be concealed so there are no distracting strings or wires. Beneath their costume, they may have partial bodies or none at all. Some types are rather simple, such as those in Guangdong Province which have a carved wooden head on an elongated neck which is inserted through a horizontal piece of wood forming the figure's shoulders. Other regions developed puppets with solid chests or torsos which give them a more convincing sense of depth and shape.

The rod puppet is supported by a large, central rod which may be nothing more than an elongated neck in some Cantonese puppets, or which may be a long wooden pole running the complete length of the figure's costume. Some rod puppets have coiled springs between the head and shoulder crossbar, permitting simple movements of the head, while other puppets have movable eyes, mouths, or ears operated by wires running down through the hollow head of the puppet.

The hands of the figure are operated by two small rods which extend below the puppet's costume. Traditionally these small rods were made of twigs or bamboo, but today wire or metal rods are more prevalent. Centuries ago, the hand rods were concealed within the costume of the puppet, so that there was less obtrusive manipulation, but a greater restriction of movement. Today exterior hand control rods have come into use. The puppet's hands

74

may be very crudely made of paper-wrapped wires twisted into two tight coils through which weapons or stage props are inserted. More commonly, however, figures have hands carved either into the shape of a fist, in the case of military characters, or with movable sections to allow the grasp and release of various stage implements.

Traditional rod puppets had no legs or feet, but in order to create more realistic movements puppeteers have learned to hold a pair of cloth legs beneath the costume and move

them to simulate walking or to suggest the knees beneath the gown of a seated rod puppet. Such movements require the services of a second puppeteer.

Regional Differences

The smallest type of rod puppet was eleven to eighteen inches high and was probably developed by itinerant performers throughout northern China. Because the puppets were small, one puppeteer could perform two roles simultaneously. This type of small rod puppet is still popular in the regions of Beijing in Hebei, and in Henan, Shandong, and Shanxi provinces.

Medium-size rod puppets measuring about thirty-six inches high were popular in Sichuan, Hunan, and Guangdong provinces, on Hainan Island, and in the cities of Yangzhou and Shanghai. During the Qing dynasty an especially ornate form of rod puppets was used in the houses of Manchu nobility in Beijing. These had ceramic or carved wooden heads and elaborate costumes. There were at one time seventy-odd troupes of this type, but by the early twentieth century, their number had dwindled to only one, which disappeared in the 1930s.

Guangdong Province has preserved two unique styles of medium-size rod puppets, one having a long central rod and the other type having only a short neck extension. These will be discussed in the next section. In the neighboring region of Hainan Island one can still see performances of a single costumed puppeteer who performs on stage with one rod puppet. No curtain is used, as both puppet and performer are integral to the drama, with the puppeteer singing and gesturing on stage as he controls the puppet.

The largest type of traditional rod puppet was almost as large as a human figure. Found in the northern part of Sichuan Province, these large puppets were called *da mu nao-ke* (large wooden skulls). They are distinctive not only for their large size, but for their fine carving and their movable eyes, eyelids, mouth, tongue, ears, and nose. Yilong County in Sichuan was especially famous for its *yin-yang* troupes which combined life-size rod puppets with performances by small children who were carried on the backs of performers. The children held the major roles in such plays and their movements and appearance were imitative of rod puppets. As such, these performances seem to represent a hold over from the "flesh puppet" performances of the Song dynasty.

Life-size rod figures are still seen today in plays with smaller rod puppets performed by the National Chinese Art Puppet Troupe in Beijing. The puppeteer supports the large figures by inserting the central rod into a holder on a large belt strapped around his waist. He manipulates the two hand rods with his own hands. The puppet has a full torso and a large central supporting rod, making it very heavy to carry. But the final effect is very striking, especially when coupled with small hand or rod puppets.

For the greatest variety of traditional types of rod puppets, one must look to the provinces of Sichuan and Guangdong. In addition to the life-size figures, Sichuan troupes used medium-size rod puppets to perform plays from Beijing opera (the most popular troupes were those of Chongqing and Chengdu). Another

Pigsy, a rod puppet controlled with interior rods.

Controlling a dancer.

Control of the rod puppet using external hand rods.

type of rod puppet seen in Sichuan was a small figure about the size of a hand puppet and used for simple one-man shows. Like the one-man rod shows of northern China, these entertainments required only a simple bag-like curtained stage which was carried on the puppeteer's shoulders during the performance of a story.

Further research into these traditional forms of rod puppet theatre in Sichuan and Guangdong provinces is certain to shed new light on its origin and development in China. It is notable that Fujian Province, so rich in hand and string puppet traditions, has never accommodated rod puppet troupes—probably precisely because the hand and string forms were too well entrenched to permit competition.

Classical Cantonese Rod Puppet Theatre

According to oral traditions of Guangdong Province, the Cantonese rod puppet theatre had its origins in the time of Ming Huang, the eighth century Tang emperor.

One of the emperor's ministers returned home to Guangdong and there he decided to recreate the music and dance performances that he had seen at the imperial court. But the people of the south were too reserved to participate in the performances, so puppets were used instead. While the legend is interesting, it is of doubtful historical value, and the actual origins of puppetry in the province have yet to be clarified. We do know that rod puppets grew to be very popular in recent centuries, as patrons competed for troupes to perform for temple fairs, village ceremonies, weddings, funerals, and important seasonal festivals. In the

nineteenth century, many Cantonese actors and puppeteers participated in the popular uprising against the Manchu government known as the Taiping Rebellion. When the rebellion was crushed in 1864, the Manchu government prohibited performances of Cantonese opera—both human and puppet—and the only way round it was to switch to performing pieces from Beijing opera. In 1911 the prohibition was lifted when the dynasty was overthrown, but by that time many of the traditional play texts of Cantonese opera had been lost and puppeteers had no recourse but to adopt plays from other sources. Further disruptions came during the two world wars, so that by the middle of the twentieth century, puppetry in the province had languished.

Two major types of rod puppet developed in Guangdong Province, each with a specific style of control in keeping with the structure of the figure. Both use the painted faces and costumes of traditional Cantonese opera.

The first type of rod puppet features a short central rod which is merely an extension of the puppet's neck. The head of the puppet is almost life-size and is hollowed out to insert controls which move the eyes and mouth. This type of puppet is manipulated by one performer, who holds the center neck rod in his right hand and manipulates the two hand rods with his left. This style of rod puppet is unique in the structure of its hand control rods, which are sharply curved inward toward the body of the puppet. This small feature creates the appearance of a solid lower arm within the costume, which is in fact empty.

The puppeteer holds his right index finger lengthwise along the neck rod, with thumb and middle finger opposing on either side. The

bottom of the central rod is about even with the puppet's waist, so that a twist of the puppeteer's palm will turn the puppet sideways or make it bow. Near the bottom of the rod is a peg to shift the eyes to right and left.

One cardinal rule of performance with this type of rod puppet is that the puppeteer must never bend the elbow of his upraised right hand, as this would cause the figure to tilt at an unnatural angle or drop beneath the normal playing level. It is very difficult to sustain the raised playing position with the right hand for long periods of time, and it is a real test of the performer's ability. If such a lapse occurs, the Cantonese audience will jeer at the puppeteer by calling out that the puppet has "fallen into the well." (Pimpaneau, p. 116) When the character has a period of no movement, however, the performer can release the hand rods and use his free left hand to support the right elbow from behind, thus relieving some of the pressure.

The puppeteer's left hand manipulates the two hand rods, with thumb and index fingers controlling one rod and the ring and little fingers, the other. The middle finger may move up or down between the two rods as needed. The control of the two rods with one hand is extremely difficult, requiring strength and dexterity to move the arm rods in different directions simultaneously.

There is an emphasis on body movement and head articulation with this type of puppet. The head moves independently of the body, as do the eyes, nose, mouth, and ears. Because these areas require greater skill in control, they are given over to the right hand.

In the hands of a master puppeteer, the rod puppet is capable of expressive and elegant

Control of the arm rods, with the left rod held stationery and only the right moving between thumb and forefinger.

Here the right rod is held stationery while the left moves.

Life-size Sichuan rod puppet used in performance by the China Art Puppet Troupe of Beijing.

One of the Immortals from the play, *Eight Immortals Cross the Ocean.*

movements. In order to create a realistic sense of vitality, the puppet is seldom held perfectly vertical but is shifted slightly forward and then backward to give a sense of lifelike movement. The gestures of male and female roles are clearly distinguished, the former displaying abrupt or violent motions of head and arms, while female characters display a slow and graceful turn of head or arms. A sense of grace and feminine shyness is conveyed as the puppet shields her face behind one of the long, trailing white sleeves of her gown while she turns her head at a slight angle for a sidelong glance. A female character may also throw her long sleeves gracefully over her shoulders and pirouette with soft, little steps.

Male and female parts are also marked by their style of walk. Male characters stride forward with a fast, rigid gait. In order to further enhance the realism of the walk, a set of separate legs is sometimes held under the costume of the puppet, especially when performing the stylized pace of a warrior who advances with toes pointing outward. The female puppet moves slowly with the merest suggestion of tiny steps. And at this point we encounter one of the most subtle aspects of the Cantonese puppet performance. The sense of a puppet's walk cannot be conveyed through the movement of the puppeteer's arms, but must be transmitted through the motions of the puppeteer himself walking backstage. For a male role, the puppeteer advances quickly, mirroring the abrupt and rigid steps of the puppet. In fact, to watch a puppeteer as he performs is to see all the emotions of the role he is creating reflected in his own movements and facial expressions. In the case of female roles, the puppeteer takes tiny steps, placing his feet directly in front of each other, which results in a gentle sway of his body and a sympathetic swaying of the body of his puppet.

Fight scenes also figure in Cantonese puppet theatre, as warriors posture and cross weapons, but they lack the realism and spirit of hand or string puppet combats.

The traditional training period required to master this form of puppetry is a three-year apprenticeship. The first step of the training involves developing the great strength and flexibility in both wrists to enable hands to be raised for long periods of time. It is also necessary to be able to judge the playing height of the puppet on stage and not to raise and lower it during performance. It is natural to want to lower the puppet for a respite, but this is a bad habit to be avoided. Sometimes, during the training period, a bamboo pole is attached beneath the main rod of the puppet in order to keep the figure at a consistent playing height. When the puppet sits or kneels, then the pole can be turned out of the way at a slant. This is only a remedial technique, however, and is used only until a student has a thorough mastery of the performing style.

In contrast to rod puppets with elongated necks, Guangdong Province also possesses a type of puppet with a complete set of shoulders and a full torso carved from one piece of wood. These are heavier and more rigid than the other style of rod puppets, and because they are carved in one piece, they do not permit movement of head or neck. Such figures are supported by a long pole which extends from the bottom of the chest or torso almost to

Another one of the Eight Immortals.

the ground. The puppeteer holds this long central rod before him, grasped in his left hand rather than in the more traditional right hand. The usual position of right and left hands is reversed in this case because of the rigid head

A scene from *The Eight Immortals Cross the Ocean*, performed by the China Art Puppet Troupe.

and body, which leave only the arms to manipulate. Therefore the right hand is used to control the arms. The construction of the controls makes other major differences in this type of puppet theatre. The puppeteer must keep elbows bent rather than fully extended because of longer rod. In addition, the hand controls are straight rather than curved; during performance, the rods are kept crossed and the puppeteer grasps them, at their intersection, with the thumb and index finger of his right hand.

Rod Puppet Troupes in China Today

Today the most famous troupe in the province is the Guangdong Puppet Troupe, established in 1956. The repertoire of the troupe includes classical plays such as *The Red Child* and *Monkey Three Times Dupes the Guardian of the Palm-Leaf Fan* based on an episode from *Journey to the West*, and *Nezha Churns up the Ocean*. Like the other puppet troupes in China, this troupe also performs a number of children's plays with social, educational or political themes. In one piece a policeman teaches children not to play in the street and to be alert for passing cars. Another play portrays a rabbit stealing the commune watermelons. An old farmer asks the children in the audience for advice about how to deal with the naughty rabbit, and encourages their various suggestions. Finally one child says to send a litle friend dressed as a scarecrow to the melon patch to catch the rabbit. When the rabbit is subsequently caught, he spouts jets of tears and asks to learn to work, too; after gentle criticism, the rabbit is taught respect for manual labor. Such children's plays are given in kindergartens, primary schools, and at nurseries set up for women factory workers. The troupe spends about equal time performing in the cities and in the countryside, where the puppeteers make the effort to use the local dialects of the region.

The most popular type of rod puppet—used by three of China's largest troupes—is about thirty to forty-two inches in length, with a solid torso and arms. Sometimes it has legs, but this depends on the movements required of the character. The hands are controlled by straight wire or metal rods which are usually external, permitting maximum ease of movement. The rod troupes using this type of figure have adopted a number of mechanical control devices and special effects to enhance the drama of their performances.

The China Art Puppet Troupe in Beijing is the national troupe of China and has over one hundred puppeteers and musicians. Since the troupe was established in 1953, fine performers from throughout the country have come to Beijing to perform with them and instruct a younger generation of puppeteers. The performing style of the troupe is eclectic, combining the best techniques of many regions rather than transmitting one local tradition. Their repertoire includes large-scale productions of classical plays such as *Monkey Creates Havoc in the Celestial Palace* from an episode in *Journey to the West* as well as plays based on Western sources such as *The Wild Swan* by Hans Christian Andersen. The troupe spends at least half of each year traveling throughout China giving performances in theatres, schools, and children's palaces.

The Shanghai Puppet Troupe performs over five hundred shows a year in kindergartens, schools, and theatres in the city of Shanghai and in other parts of the country. One of the troupe's most popular plays has been *Monkey*

A scene from *Havoc in Heaven*, performed by the China Art Puppet Troupe of Beijing.

Monkey and the Barefoot
Daoist Immortal.

Three Times Fights the White Bone Demon, based upon an episode from *Journey to the West*. This piece contains three stirring battle scenes as the protagonist fights another manifestation of the evil White Bone Demon. Another popular play, *The Ruby*, includes a number of unforget-table antagonists who reveal their true natures at strategic moments: a malevolent old demon with bulging eyes which protrude when he is angry, and a comically fat old monk who carries a small alter ego inside his huge belly. The 150 puppeteers, musicians, and craftsmen in

82

the troupe also maintain a training program for young amateur puppeteers. In 1982 there were over fifty students in this program.

The Hunan Provincial Art Puppet Troupe was established in 1956, drawing performers from many regions in the province, such as Qiyang and Longshan counties and Shaoyang District, where rod puppetry is still very popular. The troupe has some sixty plays in its repertoire, including *Monkey Three Times Fights the White Bone Demon, Tale of the White Snake, Stopping the Horse* (an historical opera set during the Song dynasty), and *The Tale of the Golden Scales*, the story of a carp fairy who falls in love with a penniless scholar. The Hunan puppeteers are especially known for their skill at stylized gestures using the long, trailing white sleeves of the classical opera costume and the pheasant tail feathers worn on the helmets of warriors, both male and female, in the opera.

中国木偶艺术

In a dark theatre in northwest China, the plaintive, sharp neigh of a horse breaks the silence. Its echoes are lost a moment later in the din of drum and gong, clapper and two-string *er-hu*, punctuated all the while by the roll of distant thunder. This is not an open-air theatre, nor is there a horse tethered backstage. These are the sounds which precede a shadow play performance, one of the most colorful and lively forms of dramatic entertainment in China.

The Chinese have always considered shadow theatre in a category of its own. Although it draws on the same body of traditional plays as the three-dimensional puppet theatres, the shadow theatre remains distinct by the fact its characters move in a two-dimensional world restricted by the boundaries of the playing screen. The gift of the shadow master is to take what appears to be a limitation and transform it into a vehicle for greater dramatic effect. He fills his screen with scenery—clouds and mountains, waves and trees, palaces and pavilions. His characters fly and spin through the air, climb trees, and cross mountains. The results are more colorful and naturalistic than any that human opera can produce with its limitations of stage and scenery.

Sound effects and special visual techniques are the dramatic extras of a shadow performance. The *suo-na*, or double-reed Chinese oboe, provides the strident neigh of a horse and striking an empty box furnishes the hoof beat. Thunder is rendered by shaking a sheet of metal, the whoosh of the wind from wood rubbed

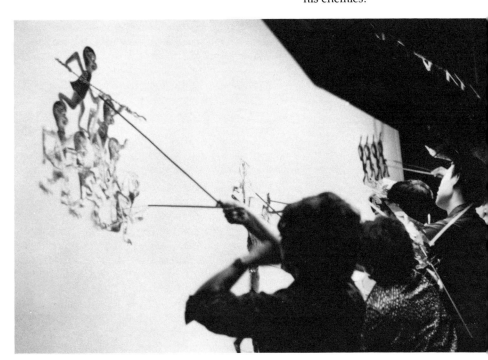

Monkey transforms himself into a cloud of small simians to confound his enemies.

SHADOW THEATRE 6

along a piece of taut silk. Because shadow characters cannot change facial expression and are restricted to life in a two-dimensional world, the shadow player uses music and song to express deep sentiments at important moments in the play. Special performing techniques also add to the force of a shadow play, whose screen, while limiting in other respects, is perfectly suited for presenting unique visual effects which cannot be duplicated in any other dramatic medium, except perhaps in animated films.

The general term for shadow theatre in China today is *pi-ying xi* or "theatre of leather shadows" because the figures are made from leather, but early on, the most widespread term for this form was *deng-ying xi*, "theatre of lantern shadows." Shadow figures have never been termed *mu-ou*, or puppet, because the Chinese have always drawn a distinction between such two-dimensional figures and three-dimensional puppets. Shadow theatre exists in almost every part of China, and is known by a different term in practically every locality. Adopted by the Communists in northwest China in the 1930s as a popular folk art suitable for educational and political work, the shadow theatre there was jokingly referred to by the local people as *tu dian-ying* or "rural cinema."

History of the Shadow Theatre

No one knows precisely when or where the shadow theatre first appeared. Some scholars argue that it was in India that shadow theatre began, and then was carried to China through central Asia on the trade routes known as the Silk Road. Others argue just as forcefully that China was the birthplace of the shadow the-atre. The final answers to such questions must await new archaeological excavations or the discovery of ancient documents that make reference to the "theatre of lantern shadows."

The legendary account of Emperor Wu, who was reunited with his dear wife through the art of shadow play, places its origins in the second century B.C., even though the date is unsupported by other literary evidence. Only in the Tang dynasty do written references to figures appear; they describe Buddhist monks using shadow figures to illustrate popular tales of the Buddha's previous lives and of the work-ing of karma. Also at this time there was the development of papercuts, intricately cut de-signs of paper, which may well be related to the birth of shadow figures. Early writers recorded that shadow figures were first constructed of white paper and that it was only later that sheepskin began to be used. A further associa-tion stems from the term *chuang-hua* (window flowers) which is used for both shadow figures and papercuts.

By the eleventh century, shadow perform-ances had achieved great popularity. In market place and on street corners shadow players en-thralled audiences with colorful, translucent figures and dramatic narrations of the lives of China's best-loved heroes and beauties. Histori-cal tales seem to have been the specialty of the shadow player, who combined fact and fiction in about equal amounts. Episodes based on *The Romance of the Three Kingdoms* were the fa-vorite of Song audiences.

Cousins to the shadow play were the *qiao-ying xi* and *da-ying xi* (theatre of large shadows) in which humans would cast silhouettes, prob-ably in imitation of the appearance and move-

Papercut showing an episode from *Monkey Three Times Fights the White Bone Demon.*

ments of shadow figures. These entertainments were particularly well liked during the period of the Song dynasty.

The popularity of shadow theatre spread in the eleventh century as the Mongols sent troupes of shadow players along with their conquering armies, and thus Chinese shadow plays were carried to Turkey, Arabia, and Egypt. By the twelfth century shadow performances had become a favorite entertainment at the court of Saladin in Egypt. In France by the mid-eighteenth century, there was an entertainment called *ombres Chinoises*, a name derived from its earliest European account by the Jesuit Father du Halde in 1735. Shortly thereafter, shadow plays took root on English soil, followed in 1774 by a German shadow performance of *Faust* arranged by Goethe.

The Ming and Qing dynasties were a great flowering period for shadow theatre, as its expansion covered the length and breadth of China, from Manchuria in the north to Guangdong in the south, and from Hebei in the east to Sichuan and Qinghai in the west. The two most important shadow schools were centered in Beijing and in Shaanxi Province. Shadow troupes performed under contract in tea houses and gave marketplace shows for a passing audience. They might also be invited to provide private entertainment on important family occasions such as betrothals, birthdays, or a childbirth. Women particularly enjoyed these private shadow performances because, since the Song dynasty, women had been increasingly sequestered within the walls of the family compound and social convention forbade any decent woman to attend a public theatre. In his book *The Adventures of Wu: The Life*

Cycle of a Peking Man, H. Y. Lowe has described the occasion of a traditional shadow play held by a Beijing family. The entire performance lasted from noon to midnight and was contracted for a sum of eight silver dollars.

While the feast was on the shadow show people got everything ready and the big glass burner of sesamum oil, suspended from a pole over the chief showman's head, was also lighted. The adjustments were made so as to get the proper distance and angle to throw the shadows on the screen properly. A musical selection served as prelude and the show started immediately with a piece from popular folklore, appertaining to the birth of a high-born child predestined to be an accomplished scholar and a successful court dignitary. The boy was supposed to have been sent by the goddesses and to have descended to earth riding a unicorn—a legendary animal, a combination of dragon and buffalo. This was the special feature in keeping with the occasion of the celebration (the son's reaching the first month of age) and was over in about seven minutes.

The program for the day was not pre-arranged or specified by the hosts and the audience was allowed, or requested, in the usual manner to choose their own favourite pieces for which privilege the time-honoured usage is for the person who chooses a piece to give a little "wine money"...

The entire repertoire is listed, name by name, on an elongated piece of bamboo plate, lacquered white and bent in a slight curve with one end somewhat narrower than the other. This is a facsimile of the ancient scepter of authority borne respectfully with both

A warrior, an official, and a mythical creature that is part deer, part dragon, part horse, and part fish. *(Collection of Diane Kempler; photo by Mary Carolyn Pindar)*

hands by high officials during imperial audiences—the original ones were made of ivory. The chief showman produced the repertoire and gave it to old Mr. Wu to pass around to the guests for their selection. "Please bestow on us your commands," Showman Li smilingly added...

Part of the guests not familiar with the shadow show were somewhat surprised at the wide range of plays presentable and which certainly did not seem possible with the comparatively small group of "operatives" in the company. There were listed between seventy and eighty plays, from one-act monologues to lengthy historical dramas such as the Three Kingdoms plays, the performance of which would take four or even five hours in the Chinese theatre. (pp. 40-1)

But the shadow player and his art came upon hard times at the end of the nineteenth century, as the Qing dynasty tottered under the twin onslaught of foreign aggression and internal rebellion. There were fewer commissions for private performances, and street corner audiences had little extra money for such entertainments. At the same time there was the competition from the recently introduced medium of films with which to contend. As a result, troupes found it increasingly difficult to support themselves and were forced to turn to other employment. When the famous ethnologist Berthold Laufer arrived in China in 1901 to carry out fieldwork and make collections for the American Museum of Natural History, he found the traditional shadow theatre of Beijing to be on the verge of extinction. In the entire city he could locate only one shadow company and only one living craftsman capable of making these figures.

I had a long talk to that man, as I first wished to order the whole material to be made new; the workman counted that it would take him at least a year and a half to accomplish the whole set, and the expenses would have

89

amounted to more than $1000 . As he is one-eyed and very old, he did not feel inclined either to undertake the task.

Laufer finally arranged to purchase the entire collection of the troupe, including musical instruments, stage curtains, dramatic texts, and more than five hundred shadow figures.

The struggle for the price lasted nearly two hours; the starting-point from which the vender descended was 1000$, while I ascended from 250$, until we agreed, in the medium, on 600$...So the ying-hsi *(shadow theatre) will soon be a matter of the past in Northern China, and I think I saved them in the last hour.* (Correspondence from Beijing dated March 1, 1902)

Laufer's prediction of the demise of the art form was somewhat exaggerated, for there were still four family troupes with some fourteen performers active in Beijing in 1912. But we can only be grateful for the foresight which brought him to obtain this valuable collection, and further, to make cylinder recordings of three of the best traditional shadow plays of that troupe.

Along with hand, string, and rod puppetry, shadow performances were encouraged by the Chinese government after 1949. Provincial and municipal troupes were established in important centers and one of their major tasks was to expand the number of performers, add new plays, and improve lighting and stage techniques. Generally speaking, there has been a tendency for greater naturalism in recent years, although the classical style has been preserved in traditional centers such as Shaanxi and Tangshan.

Special Features of the Shadow Figure

Both in size and materials, Chinese shadow figures varied greatly from region to region. In the north donkey skin was the preferred medium because of its suppleness, translucence, and durability. Cow, horse, sheep, water buffalo, and pig skins were also used depending upon the area, while poorer troupes out of necessity used bark, leaves, or a double thickness of paper for the figures, although none of the latter had the translucence of animal skin. In all cases, however, the structure of the figures remained fairly similar. The cutting and painting were done either by the performers themselves or by craftsmen who specialized in this skill.

Every region has different styles of decorating the leather for making the stock character roles, almost as hallmarks of its shadow theatre. Color is added, usually red, blue, green, and black, in addition to the natural yellow color of the processed leather. (The exact ingredients combined in the vegetable dyes were an important part of the craftsmen's repertoire to be passed down as family secrets from generation to generation.) Some types of dye cause the leather to wrinkle and so the skin has to be pressed flat after it is dyed. Finally, a coat of oil such as *wu-tong* oil is added to give durability and luster, a practice which originated in northeast China but spread quickly to most other regions.

In fashioning the figure, several choices of perspective are used in combination: profile, three-quarter, and full face. The feet are always in full profile with the legs in three-quarter, visible as separate pieces. The shoulders may be in profile or three-quarter, as may the head. Heads in full face appear to have been reserved

for special creatures, deities, and saints. This blending of various perspectives is not consciously noticed by the audience, but nevertheless adds interest to the silhouettes in spite of the limitation of their two-dimensional form. There are two types of cutting styles used for the face. In one, the majority of the facial plane is cut away, leaving only an outline of the features. In the second type, the major portion of the face is kept and only the lines detailing the features are cut away. Sometimes the two styles are combined. A face may also have movable parts manipulated by strings. Figures of Monkey and Pigsy, for example, sometimes have movable eyes and lower jaws controlled in this way. Beards of real hair are added to give a realistic touch.

The body proper is cut in ten or eleven pieces, including two hands, two forearms, two lower arms, upper torso, lower body, and two legs with feet attached—human characters rarely have fewer parts. A thinner layer of skin is used for upper sections of the figure, for lighter, easier movement. Whenever two body sections overlap, special care is taken to prevent the double thickness from adding stiffness or discoloration. All extraneous leather is cut away from the piece underneath, leaving only a spoke design behind. To keep colors from appearing darker in these places, color is applied to only the front overlapping piece. Hands might be cut in opposing sections, of thumb against the other four fingers, or with extended index and little fingers as an approximation of expressive gestures seen in the human opera. In other cases, the hands are cut into fists or in two or three movable sections.

In north and northeast China figures are relatively small, from six to ten inches, and

Carving shadow figures.

91

finely cut with intricate latticework designs. These patterns are especially striking on a woman's gown, for example, in that the interlocking motifs are so perfectly cut that even where two sections overlap, the design is unbroken. The shadow figures of central and southern China are usually larger than those of the north, and lack the detail and ornateness of northern figures.

A shadow figure moves with the aid of five-inch wire rods attached to loops at the neck and hands. At the other end of the rod is a reed handle or, more commonly, a bamboo or wooden chopstick, giving the performer better control of the rod. These three rods are adequate for creating the actions of most human characters, while animals may require fewer—one rod under the stomach or two rods at the front and rear.

Backstage Preparation

Back stage is always bustling with activity before a shadow play begins: the screen must be positioned, the lights arranged, and the shadow figures prepared. The *ying-chuang* or "shadow window" is a screen of gauzy white silk or nylon or, in some cases, paper. It is usually about five feet wide and three feet high, but may be larger in regions where bigger shadow figures are used. The screen is always slanted slightly toward the audience, which makes it easier to hold the figures flat against the playing surface. A wooden plank covered with a coarse material such as felt runs along the bottom of the screen and is used to anchor scenery and the rods of stationary characters. The stage always has a curtained area beside the playing area where scenery can be set up

Pigsy in procession followed by the Monk Xuan-zang.

and then easily slipped over into position. The figures for the performance are hung backstage from strings within easy reach of the performers. In the past, many shadow troupes had only one master player who was assisted by an apprentice, who handed him figures and took away those he was finished with. Today the tendency in China, especially among professional urban shadow troupes, is to expand the

scope of shadow plays, and with this division of labor each player must be responsible for his own figures.

Perhaps the most important part of pre-performance preparations is the placement of the lighting source. In its early development, shadow plays used vegetable oil lanterns which were later replaced by gas lamps. The traditional oil lanterns flickered, casting an unstable light, but could conceal any awkward shadows cast by the control rods which were supposed to remain invisible. Because of this, many old masters still preferred the oil lanterns, despite the advent of electric lights. And yet electricity is a more stable source and creates a brighter, clearer picture for the audience, to say nothing of doing away with the smoke and heat which were especially uncomfortable for players who had singing roles. Today fluorescent lights are preferred because of their bright but diffuse light, but if single incandescent bulbs are used, they are carefully shaded to prevent a spotlight effect on the screen. Whatever the lighting source, it is centered behind the screen at about mid-screen height, so that the light falls between the screen and the shadow players.

Control of the Figure

As with the control of three-dimensional puppets, the skill of the shadow player is acquired only after long hours of training and playing experience. Strength is not a factor so much as wrist and finger dexterity. With the left hand the player holds the central body rod supporting the body of the figure and generates body movements. With the right hand he moves the two arm rods, one of which he rolls between thumb and index finger and the other between his palm and remaining three fingers. Occasionally the legs of the shadow figure require a separate control rod, such as to hold a leg upraised. In that case, the performer takes an extra rod with a pin on the end and inserts it for temporary control of the feet. Extra rods are

Smoke signals a transformation.

always held in readiness backstage for added support of the figure for somersaults or sharp motions in fight scenes. A master shadow player is able to control up to four figures in each hand, grasping all the control bars together. Very rarely is one figure controlled by more than one performer, although in certain complicated martial scenes a second pair of hands may be required.

A common sequence in the shadow play is a procession of figures. For this, the shadow

player must hold the rods steady and at an
even height, moving the figures along in a
fluid motion but never allowing them to overlap, as this dulls color and outline. Some roles
may be stationary at times during the play, but
the experienced shadow player returns to
them often, stirring them slightly to maintain
the illusion of vitality which he has worked so
hard to create.

The audience learns the nature of the characters on stage by observing their carefully exaggerated movements, and walk is always a
key element. A female role moves with a delicate sway; the warrior advances with a bold,
quick tread; and the scholar steps with a measured gait. One secret in controlling a walk is
that the legs are usually cut in unequal lengths,
allowing them to swing more freely and overlap without sticking together. When the figure
strikes a split-leg posture, the shorter leg is always placed in front. Vigorous characters like
the Monkey King often leap up into the air,
throwing their legs apart and then switching
their position, all of which is executed just by
agitating the central rod, without the help of
extra leg rods. Elegant women and dignified
scholars move more gracefully; their bodies
roll in a natural, fluid movement as the joints of
the puppet turn slowly to sit, bow, and kneel
in a remarkably realistic manner.

Fight scenes and other movements are
carefully paced in rhythm to the musical accompaniment, but when there is a song, all
action stops. The reason for this is probably
simply that the shadow player, who sings the
songs himself, wants to concentrate on his vocal performance at those moments. Such relatively static scenes may incorporate elaborate
scenery to increase visual interest. However,

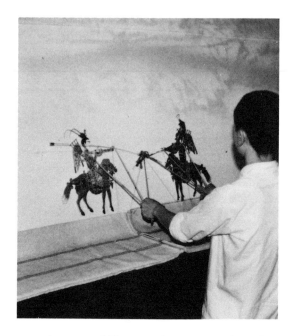

once the pace shifts to active scenes of combat
or magical transformations, the screen is usually stripped to give space for broad movements. Any scenery that does not have to be
moved during a sequence can be pinned at the
bottom of the screen for greater stability.

Perhaps the most fundamental rule of performance is that shadow figures—unless enter-
ing, exiting, or transforming—must be held flat
against the screen in order to create maximum
clarity of color and outline. With even the
slightest deviation from the screen, their outline blurs and their beautiful colors dim. Further, the shadow player must always be conscious of the placement of his rods so that they
do not cast errant shadows against the white
screen. The adoption of fluorescent, diffuse

lights has helped to avoid this problem, but even the best performer will unwittingly reveal his rods on occasion.

Special Effects of the Shadow Screen

Magical transformations, fighting scenes, and beheadings are the impressive highlights of a shadow performance. Shadow figures can drink wine, smoke a pipe, juggle, mount a horse and dismount. Fighting can be especially realistic, as the figures thrust and retreat across the screen's white space. Warriors can even launch an arrow, which is a separate prop manipulated by its own rod.

One of the most striking effects is the casting of multiple images, which are made by holding burning rods about twenty inches in back of the figure against the screen. With the addition of each burning rod, another shadow image is cast; moving the flame causes the image to move in the opposite direction. A master player can manipulate a number of these flaming sticks simultaneously until the whole screen is covered with multiple images. This is a special technique used for the Monkey King character in a dramatic moment when he transforms himself into a myriad tiny alter-egos to confound his enemies.

Through another special technique, characters make magical appearances and disappearances. By rotating the central rod of the shadow figure, the player causes the figure to turn in a 180 degree angle and, when perpendicular to the screen, it will seem to disappear for an instant, only to reappear again facing in the opposite direction. This effect is masterfully exploited when two shadow figures are placed behind the screen with one parallel to the screen and the other behind it and perpendicular to the screen. When the figure next to the screen is pulled away, the figure underneath is quickly rotated flat against the screen—seeming to appear instantaneously from nowhere.

The shadow screen is uniquely suited to suggesting natural phenomena such as wind, mist, and the movement of water. By passing steam or chemically produced smoke between the lights and the screen, the effect of clouds or flowing water is created. For the performance of *Flooding Gold Mountain Temple*, for example, this technique brings churning waves of the rising river to the screen.

In order to give the illusion of near and distant perspective, the performers use large and small figures of the same character. In some complicated plays, for example, two hundred shadow figures of different sizes are required to convey the illusion of depth, although there are only five different characters in the play.

Regional Differences

The type of shadow theatre best known to Westerners is that of northeastern China and especially of Beijing. The city serves as a dividing line between the two different styles of shadow performances that are popular. The eastern markets and areas east of the city are partial to the Luanzhou or eastern style. This type of shadow theatre uses intricately carved figures of translucent donkey skin, usually about eight inches high. During the Qing dynasty, the Manchu nobility favored this form of shadow theatre and gave such troupes considerable patronage. The form soon spread to the

The Tortoise and the Crane, a traditional shadow play performance by the Beijing Art Shadow Troupe.

neighboring provinces of Jilin and Liaoning in Manchuria. Performances usually incorporated music and singing elements from the local Beijing Opera. Most players were literate, and their performance closely followed handwritten play texts.

The shadow troupe of the city of Tangshan, in Luanzhou County where the style originated, is very well known. In 1956 there were more than twenty professional troupes in the city, and in 1980 a troupe from Tangshan performed at the Second International Shadow Theatre Festival in the French city of Charleville-Mezieres.

In the western market of Beijing and in the regions west of the city, a different style of shadow theatre prevailed, one which used larger figures of cowhide with rougher, more exaggerated lines. It was customary to use little scenery in such performances. This style of shadow theatre did not rely upon play texts, but upon the oral instructions passed down from generation to generation. For this reason, the school was also known as *liu kou ying* (shadows which flow from the mouth). The center of this theatre was in Zhuozhou, which became another name for the style.

The early years of the nineteenth century were the heyday of shadow theatre shows in the capital, but by the first half of the twentieth century, shadow figure troupes in Beijing had dwindled almost to nothing. The Cultural Revolution dealt them a further, crippling blow. But in 1983, a troupe inheriting the four-generation mantle of the Lu family came to Paris to perform a traditional repertoire to great critical acclaim. Their success is a hopeful sign that there will be renewed fame and prosperity both at home and abroad for practitioners of this age-old art.

Shaanxi Province, too, has a rich tradition of shadow performance, distinctive for its music and type of figures. Because the Silk Road trade routes ended in the bazaars of Xian in Shaanxi, some scholars argue that shadow theatre there must be the most ancient in China. There hasn't been much archaeological or written evidence to support this theory, however. Shaanxi Province has a number of different shadow troupes which differ in size of the figures and musical styles. Some regions use cowhide and others donkey skin. To the east and northeast of Xian, small six-to-eight-inch figures carved in very fine detail have been popular for centuries. Called *dong lu* or "eastern region" figures, they have a great variety of characters: one famous old carver of shadow figures has perfected over one thousand different heads. To the west of the provincial capital are found larger figures from one to two feet in height carved in a rough and vigorous style.

Shadow puppets have been very popular in Hunan Province as well. For centuries shadow plays have been performed there in village and city teahouses, where the performers' fee was paid from the sale of cups of tea. In the 1950s there were over 150 large and small shadow troupes active in Hunan. Their figures are very different from those used in northern troupes: they stand one-to-two feet tall and are constructed of paper and only rarely from leather. Using numerous sheets of paper daubed with wax, folk craftsmen cut intricate patterns to make very distinctive performing figures. In more recent years troupes have turned to leather figures because they are more

durable and easy to use.

The Hunan Art Puppet and Shadow Theatre Troupe, founded in 1956, has placed a special emphasis on the creation of lively plays with animals as the main characters. In order to enrich their various movements, the four legs of the animal figures have been connected with nylon string so that they can be moved simultaneously. One of this troupe's best known plays is a fable called *"The Tortoise and the Crane."* The troupe is also distinctive for their emphasis upon control and movement rather than music, dialogue, and song. They have introduced modern-looking figures in their performances, and many other troupes have been influenced by their experiments with larger, realistic-looking figures. Some of the traditional flavor is lost in such cases, however, and one can only hope that the old will continue to find a place next to the new rather than being replaced entirely.

In the southern Chinese provinces of Fujian and Guangdong, delicate shadow figures of colored cowhide were seen on street corners, at temple fairs, and in public squares, but the shadow player found it difficult to compete with more popular three-dimensional puppets. In the region of northern Guangdong and southern Fujian, this competition was especially sharp because of the great popularity of Fujianese hand and string puppets. Out of this competition was born a new and unique type of puppet. This new figure was seven to twelve inches tall with body of carved wood or stuffed with rice straw; the head was sculpted and painted clay. The small, elegant figures, clothed in embroidered silk costumes, were supported by a horizontal rod extending from the center of the back. Two additional thin rods controlled the two arms. These puppets probably first appeared in the 1850s, in the cities of Lufeng, Chaozhou, and Shantou in Guangdong and spread to the counties of Zhaoan and Zhangpu in Fujian. The beautiful little figures, minus control rods, were also sold at the New Year's Lantern Festival to parents who wanted to have a child or acquire a future spouse for their child. Like their shadow predecessors, the puppets were manipulated in performances that often began in the evening and lasted all night. Because the puppets were controlled just like shadow figures, this form was called "round body paper shadow theatre" (*yuan-shen zhi-ying xi*) or simply "paper shadow theatre"—not referring to the material the puppets were made of, but to the paper screen behind which the original shadow figures were manipulated.

The puppets of the "wire theatre" (*tie-xian xi*), as the form is known today, are controlled behind a stage with long silk curtains on each side to cover the performers, but with a shortened center curtain to permit the horizontal rods to pass through. The shortened curtain also allows the musicians backstage to observe movements on the stage. The puppeteer manipulates the central rod and left arm rod with his left hand and the right arm rod with his right hand; an additional rod is used when leg movements are required. For head movements, a wire with a loop is sometimes attached to the central rod. The puppets are not perfectly suited for performance, as the wooden torso is heavy and does not permit waist movements. Also the puppets cannot turn in a full circle without exposing the back rod. Yet, despite these problems, the puppets grew popular enough that by the early twentieth century they had completely displaced local shadow troupes. There are probably still small amateur troupes in the area around Shantou and Chaozhou, but Guangdong Province has had no professional troupe in the public eye since the national puppetry festival of 1955. Interestingly, the region has seen a revival of shadow theatre and shadow figures, and today there is an active professional shadow troupe in Lufeng County.

中国木偶艺术

The old retainer
drives off the devil.
*(Courtesy of Asia Society
Performing Arts Dept.)*

The types of puppet plays that are popular in China today fall into several different categories. Traditional stories from mythology, history, and literature are often performed, as are many pieces created especially for children. One typical example is the play *Hua Pi (The Painted Skin)*, adapted from a story in the collection of supernatural tales entitled *A Record of Strange Events Made at Liao Studio.*

The tales were written by Pu Songling in the 17th century. This selection from them was adapted into a puppet play by Chen Jintang of the Longxi Region Hand Puppet Troupe in 1978. I have provided my own translation of the play into English so that readers of this book may get a better understanding of the style and complexity of the Chinese puppet theatre.

Synopsis of the Story

A hideous devil, taking on the disguise of a beautiful young girl fleeing to escape from an arranged marriage, arrives at the studio of Scholar Wang, and there begins to sob piteously. Wang opens the door and, attracted by the devil-girl's beauty, invites her inside and begs her to share wine with him. The girl flirts amorously with Wang and finally gets him drunk, at which point she reveals her true features as a ferocious devil. Just as the devil is about to kill Wang, the old family retainer—who had seen through the devil's facade from the beginning—comes to Wang's rescue with a

A CHINESE PUPPET PLAY 7

Backstage look at performance of *Painted Skin*, as Chen Jintang manipulates the puppet of the scholar.

dirty old broom. He is able to beat off the demon because, according to Chinese legend, demons are afraid of dirty things. The demon disappears and only the painted skin remains.

The Play—The Painted Skin

The scene is set in a nicely furnished scholar's studio. Through the window is visible a misty landscape in dim moonlight, with a covered walk and bamboo growing nearby. As the curtain rises, Wang sits at his desk holding a book and reading by candlelight. The wind soughs in the night, and he stands up and walks to the window, drawing aside the curtain to enjoy the moonlit scene outside. He appears to be lost in a melancholy reverie.

WANG: *Reciting.*
Like water the moonlight splashes through the window. Unattached, I feel lonely in the world.
The old retainer enters, carrying a lantern in one hand and a tea tray in the other.
OLD RETAINER: *Making a bow with hands clasped.*
Master, it's late. You had better go to sleep now.
Presents tea.
WANG: *Taking the tea cup.*
You go ahead to sleep.
Waves him off.
OLD RETAINER: Yes.
The retainer leaves carrying the lantern. As he passes along the covered walk a gust of wind rises, blowing out the light and causing the old man to stagger. At the next moment, a ferocious devil appears from amid the bamboo groves. The old retainer hurries off.

DEMON: *Laughing.*
Ha! Ha! Ha!
Yells suddenly.
Change!
*Shrouded in a cloud of blue smoke, the devil transforms himself into a bewitchingly beautiful lady. The lady walks on tiptoe to the window of the study, peers around her, and then gently knocks at the window. Seeing Wang sound asleep at his desk, she picks up a pebble and tosses it inside.
Wang wakes up with a start and glances around. Seeing nothing there, he sits down again to read. Outside the window, the lady begins to weep, clutching a handkerchief while Wang listens thoughtfully at the window. As he opens the door to see who is crying, the lady hurries off into the bamboo grove.*
WANG: *Looks around and finds the lady crying among the bamboos.*
Oh!
Goes forward and greets her.
Miss...
*The lady turns her head away shyly.
Stunned by her beauty, Wang speaks in an aside to the audience.*
Ah! She is indeed a great beauty.
He steals sidelong glances at her, as the lady deliberately turns her head away.
WANG: Miss, may I ask what makes you so unhappy that you cry here in the middle of the night?
BEAUTY: You cannot relieve this sorrow since you are a stranger. Why do you bother to ask?
WANG: Please tell me and I will do anything I can to help you.
BEAUTY: *Pretending shy hesitation.*
Well...

Sings.
This is all because of my unreasonable parents who wanted to marry me off as a concubine into a rich family; lamenting my ill fate, I left home to escape the marriage.
WANG: So that's it. But where will you go now?
BEAUTY: I have nowhere to go and no relatives to turn to. How miserable I am!
Weeps again.

"Painted Skin" performance.

WANG: Miss, don't be so sad. Would you like to rest for a while in my study and then we'll see what can be done for you?
BEAUTY: Please.
Wang and the Beauty walk into the study.
WANG: *Fills a cup with tea and brings it to the Beauty.*
Miss, please have some tea.
BEAUTY: Thank you, young scholar.
Reaches out and takes the cup, but purposefully lets the cup slip from her hands.
Oh, no!

The devil threatens the scholar, from *The Painted Skin. (Courtesy of Asia Society Performing Arts Dept.)*

Wang and the Beauty both bend down to pick up the cup. The Beauty then pretends to trip and fall.

WANG: Oh, my!

Helps the Beauty to rise. Are you hurt?

BEAUTY: No, I'm not. Thank you for your help.

Turns away shyly, but soon casts amorous glances at Wang. Infatuated, Wang stares at the beauty, who poses and then feigns shyness.

WANG: *Flustered.*

Miss, please, please sit down.

Moving a stool over and cleaning it with his sleeve to indicate his sincerity.

Please sit down.

The Beauty thanks him and sits down. She reaches over to pluck the strings of the classical qin *stringed instrument on the scholar's desk.*

Shall your humble servant play some music to lighten your spirits?

BEAUTY: *Giving a winsome smile.*

How shall I repay your kindness, dear one?

Wang plays the instrument, while the Beauty smiles coquettishly.

BEAUTY: Bravo! The melody is so beautiful.

WANG: You know music well. What a pity I didn't meet you sooner...

BEAUTY: *Presses Wang's hands on the instrument with seeming shyness.*

Pardon me for my boldness. May I dare ask you to teach me to play?

WANG: With pleasure!
Holds her hands to guide her fingers on the strings. Sings.
The bright moon shares my deep feelings;
What joy to find one who understands my innermost thoughts.

BEAUTY: *Sings.*
Deeply moved by your feelings,
I shall be your companion all my life.
The Beauty presses against Wang tightly.
The old retainer is about to enter the study, but on seeing the two, he hurriedly turns back.
Wang plays the qin *again with great interest as the beauty dances alluringly.*

WANG: Old retainer, bring wine for us!
The old retainer brings wine and some dishes of food into the studio. He pulls Wang aside.

RETAINER: Young Master, it is the depth of night, and we don't know this lady at all...

WANG: *Angrily.*
Don't be so suspicious. Leave us.

RETAINER: *Trying to persuade Wang again.*
Young master, young master!

WANG: Do not say one more word; just get out!
Flings out his long sleeves in dismissal and turns to walk closer to the Beauty.
The old retainer exists, shaking his head helplessly. Angrily.
Damn, what an annoyance that man is!

BEAUTY: *Ingratiatingly.*
The servant is only rather stupid. Don't take it to heart. Here!
Raising the cup.
Let me respectfully offer you some wine.

She raises the jar of wine and forces him to empty it.

WANG: Ha, ha, ha!
Sways drunkenly.
O, Oh!
Wang falls down in a drunken stupor, and the Beauty helps him onto the bed.

WANG: *Mumbling.*
Beautiful lady, beautiful lady, come to bed quickly...
The Beauty glances about her and then utters an unnatural laugh. As a cloud of blue smoke appears, the painted skin falls off and the Beauty suddenly resumes her true demon form.

DEMON: *Seizing Wang by the collar.*
Scholar Wang, I have you now!

WANG: *Awakening with a start.*
No!

DEMON: *Laughing coldly.*
Your life is finished!
Wang falls down in terror. As he struggles to get up, his cap drops off. He spins his long hair in fright and flaps his sleeves, begging the demon to let him go. Laughing loudly, the demon advances upon Wang, who retreats and hides under a table, where he is caught by the demon. The demon opens its horrible mouth to eat the scholar's heart... Just then the old retainer forces open the window and jumps inside. He tosses a chair at the demon, who dodges it. The retainer suddenly gets an idea. He grabs a broom, and beats the demon repeatedly. The demon cries out in fear, and suddenly disappears in a cloud of smoke, leaving behind only the painted skin of a beautiful woman.

WANG: A painted skin!

RETAINER: Are you alright, young master?

WANG: *Bowing to the old man.*
I owe my life to you!
Curtain.

With their detailed carving and careful painting, Chinese puppets are objects of art in their own right. A combination of the great classical Chinese skills of carving, painting, and embroidery, puppets are the products of close cooperation between the professional craftsman and the puppeteer. Puppet making is a demanding skill, as the figures must not only suit the specific requirements of individual performers, but also be faithful to traditional roles rural and urban. Because of this every character is immediately recognizable to both audiences in China.

Indeed, every master puppeteer knows the debt of gratitude owed to the craftsmen who have created his puppets—puppets that obey the slightest twitch of the fingers, that have haunting expressions and beautiful costumes. We can appreciate the skill and work that go into every Chinese puppet by looking first at the two essential crafts involved in puppet making: carving and embroidery. Then, with a description of the methods used by the Chinese in creating their figures, we have included suggestions for making them using western materials. The shadow figure explained here in a simplified version makes an excellent first project by not being overly detailed and yet allowing some fun and experimentation. Sources for further reading are cited for those who would like more detailed instruction. By all means, try your own designs and ideas for materials and staging.

HOW TO MAKE A CHINESE PUPPET

Zhangzhou puppet carver, Xu Zhuchu, working on a hand-puppet head.

The Skill of the Carver

The puppet carvers of Fujian have historically been the most respected and their hand puppets the most sought after in all of China. Their craft was greatly influenced by the long tradition of religious sculpture, so that many of their puppets carry certain details of Buddhist images.

To learn the art of puppet carving, an apprentice studies about five years—as much time as the apprentice puppeteer devotes to learning his craft. Like puppeteers, carvers often begin their study in a family environment where skills are passed down from generation to generation.

One of the best known master carvers is Jiang Jiazou, a native of Quanzhou. Jiang used two kinds of wood for the puppet head and hands: camphor wood is, in southern China, the most desirable material because it is fine-grained, lightweight, and not easily cracked; it also has a light fragrance which repels insects and reduces sweaty odors produced in a performance. Jiang also used pearwood which is hard and fine-grained but also more difficult to carve and will not deter insects.

Within a sphere just two-and-one-half-inches in diameter, an artist must convey a total sense of character. To do this, certain special techniques have been developed in Fujian, such as exaggerating the mouth, eyes, and silhouette. Jiang was the first carver to actually identify the essential elements that characterize good or evil: the five features (*wu-xing* or two eyes, two nostrils, and mouth) plus three bones (*san-gu*, or the eye ridge, cheekbone, and jawbone). He also would carve his puppet heads at a slight angle, so that the audience seated below the stage could see them to their best advantage. Of the 280 characters Jiang created, many were modeled on the tradespeople he knew; a water carrier and a snack vendor are two very popular ones.

Perhaps the most interesting discovery has become the specialty of fourth generation carver Xu Niansong of Zhangzhou. He slightly extends the ridges above the puppet's eyes and mouth, so that these features are visible when viewed from below, but not from above. As a result, the puppet appears to change expression simply by the angling up or down of the head.

The carving of a head can take four or five days or several weeks. After the head is completely carved, painted, and polished, hats and headdresses of human hair are added. This last touch was a special skill of Jiang Jiazou, who invented twenty different styles for braided hair alone. In every detail, his puppets are exquisite works of art.

The carving of the hands for a puppet also takes much skill. The hands are often shaped into fists with a small hole in them so that they can hold flags, swords, fans, and other props. Hands are also frequently divided into two sections with the fingers joined to the palm by a metal pin so that the hands will fall open when turned palms up.

The Skill of the Embroiderer

Silk production, weaving, and embroidery have long been traditional Chinese skills. At least eight embroidery stitches were in use by the Han dynasty, and today, there are easily over forty.

The embroiderer's task is no less important than that of the carver because once on stage, the puppet and its costume vie for the audience's attention. The first step is to transfer a design to cloth, usually silk, while it is held taut in a frame; the embroiderer uses either a paper pattern or stencils to do this. Embroidery is selected to decorate the costume at the hem, sleeves, and neck. Frequently, one finds couching stitches and applique work as

touches for the front panel of the costume, and even imitation jewels may be set into the material. When the design work is completed, the pieces are cut out and the costume sewn together.

Costumes must denote character to the audience; the embroiderer adheres to traditional colors and styles. Scholarly officials are generally clothed in pastel colors; virtuous women wear pale shades, while coquettes are dressed in eye-catching hues. Long trailing sleeves of silk gauze are added to identify elegant women or scholars. But the most richly embroidered costumes are those of the warriors, which often contain animal designs with extra padding and couching.

Making a Hand Puppet

In the traditional process the head is made first. The wood must be hollowed out to exactly fit the index finger of the puppeteer who will use the figure. After the shaping and carving of the features, a coat of varnish made of local yellow clay and glue is applied in ten or more coats to help form and shape the head; in between coats, layers of soft, durable paper made from mulberry bark are applied to give the clay additional support, followed by repeated polishing. The faces are then painted on, conforming to the colors and designs of human opera but more exaggerated to make them more visible. One more polishing with paraffin and the finished head is smooth and glossy.

The puppet is then turned over to the embroiderer for costuming and assembly.

To make your own hand puppet, it might be easier to shape the head, hands, and feet

Sculpted and painted hand puppet head.

Pattern for a hand puppet.

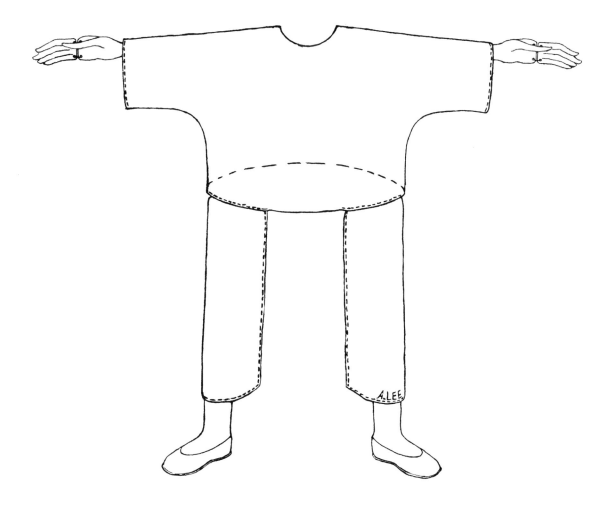

Body of a hand puppet.

General's costume.

from clay or papier mâché instead of wood. Make the neck and head of equal length, about one-and-one-half inches, and remember to hollow them out to fit your hand. The costume may be made of something as simple as muslin, in a loose style shaped with foam or padding; the costume should cover your hand with thumb and middle finger outstretched as the puppet's arms and the forefinger inserted into the head. Glue hands to the cuffs and attach feet to a pair of stuffed cotton legs which are glued in the front of the costume at the waist. Paint on a face and add yarn hair before glueing the neck well inside the collar of the costume.

Further information about making hand puppets and staging hand puppet plays can be found in Esme McLaren's *Making Glove Puppets* (Boston: Plays Inc., 1973).

Making a String Puppet

Marionettes from Fujian Province are various sizes, some up to three feet tall. The heads are carved of camphor wood as is traditional, but the torso is now shaped with twisted wire rather than bamboo, hemp, or other natural material. Limbs have evolved to have elbow and knee joints and are now largely made of foam plastics. The strings have also changed over the centuries, becoming both longer and more numerous. They are attached to the puppet and then tied to a wooden control piece that may be shaped like a cross, T-bar, "I," or rectangle.

You will find string puppets to have the most complicated structure of all and require the most time to construct. For the torso, sew an elongated casing out of muslin, stuff with

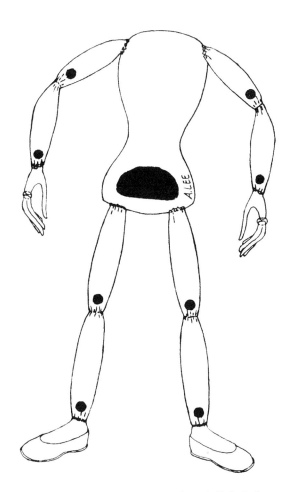

Body of a marionette.

paper or foam, and sew it closed. Fabric legs and arms will move more realistically if small weights are attached at all of the joints (wrists, elbows, knees, ankles) and below the waist (see illustration). Attach limbs and a clay or papier mâché head to the body. After you have added a costume, the figure is ready to string.

113

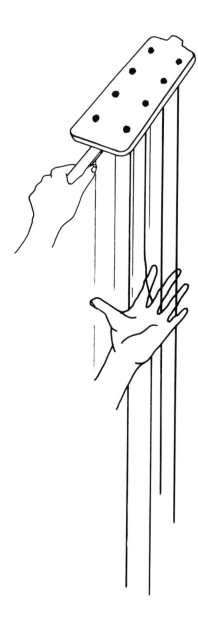

Strings attached to marionette control.

For a control, drill eight holes along the sides of a thin piece of wood (see illustration). One that is five inches long is ample for a three-foot figure. Knot strings through the holes and attach to figure at the head, shoulders, wrists, and feet. Additional holes and strings can be added for controlling the knees, calves, and elbows of the puppet.

Further information about making string puppets and staging marionette plays can be found in Helen Fling's *Marionettes, How to Make and Work Them* (Mineola, N.Y.: Dover, 1973).

Making a Rod Puppet

The most commonly seen rod puppet in China today is about thirty to forty-two inches tall and held by the puppeteer on a long pole. The head and neck are carved as one piece, with the neck elongated to serve as the torso. The costume joined at the neck will have hands attached to the sleeves that are either fist-shaped or jointed, depending on the character being made. Legs as separate pieces are made only for certain puppet roles.

To control movement, straight wire or metal rods are attached at the wrists on the outside of the costume, making them quite visible to the audience. Additional wires which operate the eyes, mouth, or ears are run through the hollow head and down the torso or main support rod.

Rod puppets have probably the simplest structure among the four types of Chinese figures as they lack a real body and legs. They are supported by a stick, or central rod, that can be made from a l-inch dowel or a broom handle. The length will depend on how tall the puppet must be for the height of your puppet

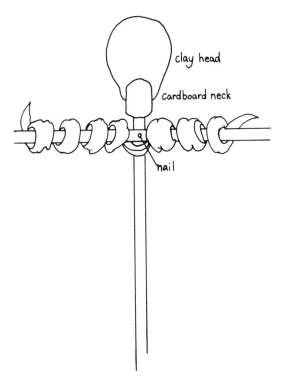

clay head

cardboard neck

nail

made of clay or stuffed muslin to the ends of the sleeves.

The control bars are added last. Make two long rods by straightening out two wire clothes hangers. Bend a small loop at one end of each rod and sew the loops to either hand.

Further information about making rod puppets can be found in Hansjurgen Fettig's *Hand and Rod Puppets* (Boston: Plays Inc., 1973).

Making a Shadow Figure

The first shadow figures known to exist were cut from plain paper; eventually more durable material such as animal skins was used and given bright colors.

Leather continues to be used today, decorated with cut-out designs and beautiful dyes. The process of construction can take several days, depending on the complexity of the figure and its designs. The skin must be soaked in water, stretched, and dried before it is cut into thin layers and polished. Patterns are then transferred onto the skins by perforation. The leather is then cut out over a frame that is, interestingly, the same type used in making papercuts.

The body consists of ten or eleven pieces modeled on the human body, and cut out to slightly overlap. The overlapping pieces are tied together with string, but not too tightly to impede movement. Almost all heads are made interchangeable and are inserted into a leather band at the top backside of the torso.

For further information, see Lotte Reiniger's *Shadow Theatres and Shadow Films* (London: Batsford Ltd., 1970).

Here are some instructions for making a very simple shadow figure.

stage. Attach a cross slat of wood to the central rod (see illustration) with wood glue or nails that are thin enough so as not to split the dowel rod. To shape the puppet's shoulders, wrap sections of fabric or foam rubber around the cross slat and secure these pieces of cloth or foam rubber with staples.

The head can be made from clay or papier mâché; its neck should have a hollow opening large enough to fit over the end of the central rod. It can be stapled or glued in place. Paint and decorate the head, and make a muslin gown that has long sleeves; glue costume to the head at the neck. Glue or sew small hands

MAKING YOUR OWN SHADOW FIGURE

Materials:

Graph paper or tracing paper

Matte mylar or matte acetate, sold by the
sheet (25" x 40") or roll. Thickness
should be at least .003.

Scissors

Coloring : felt pens, watercolors, or
colored pencils

Clear varnish (a spray varnish is available
at art stores)

Embroidery or darning needle and
heavy-duty thread

Glue

Two wire hangers, or 2-3 feet of 18-gauge
wire

Steps 1 & 2. Choosing and Drawing a Pattern:

Our example (Fig. 1) is from Beijing.
Note how the face is in full profile while the
body is almost a three-quarter pose. To reproduce to scale, redraw the pattern pieces
(Fig. 2) on graph paper, allowing 1 square: 1
inch. Other inspirations for shadow figures
can be taken from books, plays, or your own
imagination, but for your first attempt, keep
the figure simple.

The pattern pieces shown allow for some
overlap (note the extra margins around the
ends that will be joined). On your own designs, too, it is a good idea to experiment on
paper before you start on the acetate.

Lay patterns upside down on the matte or
rough side of the acetate and trace around
them with a pencil or pen. Cut out. For an
authentic touch, in the places that will be
covered by an overlapping piece, cut out
wedges of acetate, staying well inside the
edges and leaving a crosspiece of acetate at

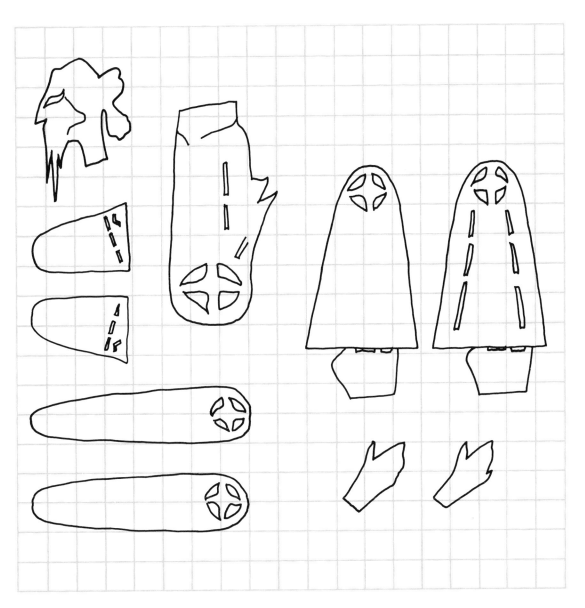

Pattern for a shadow
fig.2

117

The neck of the shadow figure fits into the collar piece. fig. 3

Attaching the rod to the shadow figure's hand. fig. 4

the center. This will help minimize a shadow effect.

Step 3. Coloring and Varnish

Working on the matte side, fill in color and outline features using whatever color method you choose. Be careful not to touch the vellum or acetate with dirty or greasy fingers or the color will not stick. For other traditional Chinese designs, refer to the illustrations throughout this book.

To set the color and design, spray or brush on a thin coat of varnish. Allow to dry.

Step 4. Assembling

Make a small hole with the needle in all pieces where they join other parts. Thread the needle with a double strand of thread, knot the ends, and pull thread through the two joining pieces; knot snugly on the other side. Cut thread and repeat at each joint.

To attach the head to the torso, first join the ends of the collar piece and, flattening, glue to the top of the torso, on the back side. The neck slides into this collar (Fig. 3).

Step 5. Attaching the Rods

Again use a needle to make holes in the hands and neck for attaching the rods. Bend each length of wire into a small loop at one end and attach this loop with thread through the holes in the figure (Fig. 4).

Step 6. Stage and Lighting

Compared to other kinds of theatre, the shadow figure theatre requires very little equipment; a screen and light source are really all that is necessary.

A cotton bedsheet can serve as the screen. It should be stretched and tacked to a frame—a wooden doorway is adequate. If your audience is going to sit on the floor, center the screen just at their eye level, or slightly above.

The light can come from various sources, but the stronger it is, the more dramatic the effect. A 40-watt bulb will be effective 24" to 32" from the screen. A slide projector can also be used to provide the light. Generally, the light should be centered behind the screen and above the puppeteer. But the height and angle will depend on where the audience sits and the size of your figures.

A very good source for staging a shadow figure performance is Nancy H. Cole's *Puppet Theatre in Performance* (New York: Morrow, 1978).

118

GLOSSARY OF TERMS

白蛇传	*Bai She Zhuan*	"The Tale of the White Snake," a popular drama which recounts the love of a serpent spirit for a scholar
八字	*ba-zi*	"character eight," describing a male dramatic gait with toes pointed outward like the Chinese character for eight
北派	*bei-pai*	"northern school," referring to the school of hand puppetry centered around the city of Zhangzhou in Fujian Province.
扁担戏	*bian-dan xi*	"shoulder pole theatre," denoting the small hand puppet stage of northern China
丑	*chou*	traditional comic roles of Chinese theatre, portraying characters deficient in some important aspect of their personality
窗花	*chuang-hua*	"window flowers," denoting both papercuts and shadow figures
大木脑壳	*da mu nao-ke*	"large wooden skulls," denoting life-size rod puppets of Sichuan Province
大影戏	*da-ying xi*	"theatre of large shadows," probably with human actors to cast silhouettes rather than shadow figures
旦	*dan*	traditional category of female roles in Chinese opera and puppet performances
灯影戏	*deng-ying xi*	"theatre of lantern shadows"
顶手	*ding-shou*	"upper hand," term for assistant hand puppeteer
东路	*dong lu*	"eastern region"
二胡	*er-hu*	two-string Chinese instrument
二手	*er-shou*	"second hand," term for assistant hand puppeteer

方相氏	*fang-xiang shi*	an exorcist officiating at ancient ceremonies held before the new year to drive away pestilence and evil influences
棍举木偶	*gun-ju mu-ou*	"rod-held puppets," denoting rod puppets
火焰山	*Huo-yen Shan*	"Mountain of Fire," an episode from *Journey to the West*
嘉礼戏	*jia-li xi*	"theatre of auspicious rituals," traditional term for the marionette theatre of the Quanzhou region of Fujian Province
净	*jing*	traditional "painted face" roles of Chinese opera and puppet performances, usually portraying warriors or statesman
傀儡	*kui-lei*	earliest term for puppets
傀儡调	*kui-lei diao*	"puppet music," a type of soft, southern music developed to accompany Quanzhou marionette performances
立子戏	*li-zi xi*	"standing theatre," referring to hand puppet stage of northern China
练功	*lian-gong*	practice exercises
流口影	*liu kou ying*	"shadows which flow from the mouth," denoting the shadow theatre of western Beijing and the counties west of the city
闽南话	*min-nan hua*	the local dialect of southern Fujian Province
木偶	*mu-ou*	modern term for three-dimensional puppets, not used for shadow figures
木偶化	*mu-ou hua*	"puppetization," or changing into a puppet style
南派	*nan-pai*	southern school of hand puppetry centered around the city of Quanzhou, Fujian Province.
皮影戏	*pi-ying xi*	"theatre of leather shadows"
乔影戏	*qiao-ying xi*	"theatre of tall shadows," probably with human actors casting silhouettes rather than shadow figures
肉傀儡	*rou kui-lei*	"flesh puppets," referring to type of Song Dynasty puppet, possibly a type of hand puppet or a performance with small children

120

水满金山	**Shui Man Jin Shan**	"Flooding Gold Mountain Temple," a popular episode from "The Tale of the White Snake"
生	*sheng*	traditional category of male roles in Chinese opera and puppet performances
手托戏	*shou-tuo xi*	"hand-supported theatre," meaning rod puppet theatre
唢呐	*suo-na*	reed musical instrument
铁线戏	*tie-xian xi*	"wire theatre," modern term for horizontal rod puppet theatre
通	*tong*	"through," with the implication of being inside or hidden
头手	*tou-shou*	"leading hand"
土电影	*tu dian-ying*	"rural cinema"
托戏	*tuo xi*	"palm-supported theatre," meaning rod puppet theatre
文	*wen*	"civil," referring to plays on non-military themes
西游记	*Xi-you Ji*	Journey to the West, a popular cycle of legends describing the pilgrimage of the famous Buddhist monk Xuan-zang, who travelled to India in the 7th century.
武	*wu*	"martial," referring to plays with swordplay and acrobatics
武功	*wu-gong*	the skill of performing acrobatics and martial arts in battle scenes
五形三骨	*wu-xing san-gu*	"the five features and three bones," important facial elements to be emphasized in carving a puppet head, according to famous artist Jiang Jiazou
下手	*xia-shou*	"lower hand," term for an assistant hand puppeteer
学戏	*xue-xi*	teaching operas through which young puppeteers learn to master essential movements
阴阳	*yin-yang*	in Chinese puppetry, this term denotes puppet troupes in Yilong County, Sichuan Province, who combined life-size rod puppets with performances by small children carried on the shoulders

影窗	*ying-chuang*	"shadow window," the screen for a shadow performance
影戏	*ying-xi*	"shadow theatre"
俑	*yong*	figures of humans, made of wood, clay or straw, placed in a tomb to serve the master in the afterlife
圆身纸影戏	*yuan-shen zhi-ying xi*	"round body paper shadow theatre," denoting horizontal rod puppet theatre of Chaozhou and Shantou in Guangdong Province and Zhaoan and Zhangpu Counties of Fujian
杖头傀儡	*zhang-tou kui-lei*	"staff-head puppet," denoting rod puppets
杖头木偶	*zhang-tou mu-ou*	"staff-head puppet," denoting rod puppets

BIBLIOGRAPHY

This section is a selected bibliography of useful works about Chinese puppetry and shadow theatre. Not included are works about Chinese drama in general or types of puppetry in other countries.

As elsewhere in this book, Chinese terms have been transcribed in *Pinyin* romanization, but with hyphens used to indicate syllables of meaningful units.

WORKS IN WESTERN LANGUAGES

Batchelder, Marjorie. *Rod-Puppets and the Human Theater.* Columbus: Ohio State University Press, 1947.

Broman, Sven. *Chinese Shadow Theatre.* Monograph Series No. 15. Stockholm: Ethnographical Museum of Sweden, 1981.

Dolby, William. "The Origins of Chinese Puppetry," *Journal of the School of Oriental and African Studies,* 41, 1, 97-120.

Ge Hong (Ke Hung). *Alchemy, Medicine and Religion in the China of A.D. 320: The Nei P'ien of Ke Hung (Pao-p'u tzu).* Tr. and ed. by James Ware. New York: Dover reprint, 1981.

Helstein, Melvyn, *et al. Asian Puppets.* Catalogue of exhibition at the Museum of Cultural History of the University of California at Los Angeles, 1976.

Humphrey, Jo. *Monkey King: A Celestial Heritage.* Catalogue of St. John's University exhibition, 1980.

Kagan, Alan. *Cantonese Puppet Theater: An Operatic Tradition and its Role in the Chinese Religious Belief System* (unpublished Ph.D. dissertation, Indiana University, 1978).

Komroff, Manuel, ed. *The Travels of Marco Polo.* New York: Modern Library, 1953.

Laufer, Berthold. *Oriental Theatricals.* Chicago: Field Museum of Natural History, 1923.

Lowe, H.Y. *The Adventures of Wu: The Life Cycle of a Peking Man.* Princeton: Princeton University Press, 1983.

Obraztsov, Sergei. *The Chinese Puppet Theatre.* Boston: Plays, Inc., 1975.

Pimpaneau, Jacques. *Des Poupée à l'Ombre.* Paris: Centre de Publication Asie Orientale, 1977.

Schipper, Kristofer. "The Divine Jester: Some Remarks on the Gods of the Chinese Marionette Theater," *Bulletin, Institute of Ethnology,* Academica Sinica (Taipei), No. 21 (Spring 1966), 81-97.

Shadow Figures from the Collection of Pauline Benton. Catalogue of Minnesota Museum of Art, 1971.

Stalberg, Roberta. "China's Great Puppet Tradition—A Backstage Look," *The Puppetry Journal,* March/April 1982, 15-8.

——————— . "Berthold Laufer's China Campaign," *Natural History Magazine,* 92, 2 (February 1983), 34-9.

——————— . *Puppetry of China.* Catalogue of exhibition with the Center for Puppetry Arts, 1984.

Tian Han. *The White Snake.* Tr. by Yang Xianyi and Gladys Yang. Beijing: Foreign Languages Press, 1957.

Werle, Helga. "Swatow (Ch'aochow) Horizontal Stick Puppets," *Journal of the Royal Asiatic, Hong Kong Branch,* 1973, 73-84.

Wu Chengen. *Monkey.* Tr. by Arthur Waley. New York: Grove Press Inc., 1958.

Young, Conrad Chun Shih. *The Morphology of Chinese Folk Stories Derived from Shadow Plays of Taiwan* (unpublished Ph.D. dissertation, University of California, Los Angeles, 1971).

WORKS IN CHINESE

Chen Dexing. "Quanzhou ti-xian mu-ou yi-shu fa-zhan shi chu-tan" (Preliminary Survey into the History of the Development of Quanzhou's Marionette Theatre), *Quanzhou wen-shi* (Literature and History of Quanzhou), 23 (June 1980), 68-91.

Fujian gong-yi mei-shu xuan-ji (Collection of Crafts of Fujian). Fuzhou: People's Press of Fujian, 1959.

Fujian xi-qu ju-zhong (Dramatic Genres of Fujian). Fuzhou: Fujian Provincial Drama Research Institute, 1981.

Geng Kefei, ed. "Zhong-guo de pi-ying yi-shu" (The Art of China's Shadow Theatre), *Fine Arts of China*, Spring 1980, 65.

_____, ed. "Lu Jingda yu Beijing pi-ying" (Lu Jingda and the Beijing Shadow Theatre), *Fine Arts of China*, Spring 1980, 65-6.

Jiang Jiazou mu-ou diao-ke (The Puppet Carvings of Jiang Jiazou). Shanghai: People's Fine Arts Press, 1958.

Jin Weinuo. "Zhang Xiong fu-fu mu-yong yu chu-Tang kui-lei xi" (Funerary Figures from the Tomb of Zhang Xiong and his Wife and [Their Connection with] Early Tang Puppetry), in *Zhong-quo mei-shu shi lun-ji* (Collected Articles on Chinese Art History). Beijing: People's Fine Arts Press, 1981.

Sun Kaidi. *Kui-lei xi kao-yuan* (Research into the Origins of the Puppet Theatre). Shanghai: Shang-za Press, 1952.

Wu Meiping. "Shaanxi pi-ying" (The Shaanxi Shadow Theatre), *Fine Arts of China*, Spring 1980, 66.

Yang Feng and Ma Mingquan. "Mu-ou yi-shu gui-lü chu-tan" (Preliminary Investigation into the Rules of Puppetry), draft manuscript, n.d.

Yang Yazhou. "Yi fu-qin—Yang Sheng" (Recollections about My Father—Yang Sheng), *Fujian xi-ju* (Drama of Fujian), 4 (1981), 22-4.

Yu Zheguang. *Pi-ying xi yi-shu* (Art of the Shadow Theatre). Shanghai: Cultural Press, n.d.

_____. *Mu-ou xi yi-shu* (The Art of Puppetry). Shanghai: Cultural Press, 1957.

INDEX